PENGUIN REFERENCE

PHANTOM HITCHHIKERS AND DECOY DUCKS

Albert Jack nailed his colours to the mast with his huge bestsellers *Red Herrings and White Elephants* and *Shaggy Dogs and Black Sheep*. The books had long-term serials in the *Sunday Times* and the *Sunday Telegraph* respectively and Albert became a regular feature on TV and Radio. Now he has turned his detective skills to urban legends, and to finding out the great stories behind the stories we can't stop telling each other.

Renowned for his own tall tales, Albert insists that not all of what he writes is bollocks. And he has recently admitted that his middle name (Hercules) has more to do with *Steptoe and Son*'s carthorse than the demigod . . .

www.albertjack.com

PHANTOM HITCHHIKERS AND DECOY DUCKS

The Strange Stories Behind the Urban Legends We Can't Stop Telling Each Other

Albert Jack

Illustrator: Sandra Howgate

PENGUIN BOOKS

PENGUIN BOOKS

Published by the Penguin Group
Penguin Books Ltd, 80 Strand, London WC2R ORL, England
Penguin Group (USA) Inc., 375 Hudson Street, New York, New York 10014, USA
Penguin Group (Canada), 90 Eglinton Avenue East, Suite 700, Toronto, Ontario,
Canada M4P 2Y3 (a division of Pearson Penguin Canada Inc.)
Penguin Ireland, 25 St Stephen's Green, Dublin 2, Ireland
(a division of Penguin Books Ltd)
Penguin Group (Australia), 250 Camberwell Road, Camberwell,
Victoria 3124, Australia (a division of Pearson Australia Group Pty Ltd)
Penguin Books India Pvt Ltd, 11 Community Centre,
Panchsheel Park, New Delhi – 110 017, India
Penguin Group (NZ), 67 Apollo Drive, Rosedale, North Shore 0632,
New Zealand (a division of Pearson New Zealand Ltd)
Penguin Books (South Africa) (Pty) Ltd, 24 Sturdee Avenue,
Rosebank, Johannesburg 2196, South Africa

Penguin Books Ltd, Registered Offices: 80 Strand, London WC2R ORL, England

www.penguin.com

First published in hardback as *That's Bollocks!* 2006
Reissued in paperback as *Phantom Hitchhikers and Decoy Ducks* 2008
1

Copyright © Albert Jack, 2006
Illustrations copyright © Sandra Howgate, 2006
All rights reserved

Albert Jack supports the MacKinnon Trust, a registered charity working to raise
public awareness about mental health issues such as schizophrenia and the care
needed by those who suffer and their families: *www.mackinnontrust.org*

Albert Jack's website is *www.albertjack.com*

The moral right of the author has been asserted

Set in Adobe Sabon
Typeset by Rowland Phototypesetting Ltd, Bury St Edmunds, Suffolk
Printed in England by Clays Ltd, St Ives plc

ISBN: 978-0-141-03851-3

www.greenpenguin.co.uk

This book is dedicated to the memory of Lord Stratford (Tony Banks) and David Bonnie, who sadly passed away while I was compiling these tales. Both of them were dear friends of mine and are sadly missed.

Contents

Acknowledgements

Thanks in the first place to Peter Patsalides for all the help this year, and also to good friends Paul Ryan and Paul Richardson who, in conversation over lunch on the Isle of Dogs when we were discussing potential ideas for a new book, suggested a study of urban legends. So this is all their fault.

Special thanks must go to the Penguin team of Ellie Smith, Georgina Laycock and Jodie Greenwood (editorial), Kate Parker (copy-editing) and Preena Gadher (marketing) and to Sandra Howgate for the fantastic illustrations.

Others who have contributed ideas, research material, suggestions and support along the way include Peter Blow, Paul Cockerham, Denise Hance, Tony Henderson, Joe Hobbs, Andy McDaniel, Melanie Tranter and especially John Riley for keeping me alive on the great drive through Africa in December 2005. Huge thanks to Janél Welgemoed and Greg Powell for taking care of me in Cape Town, and as usual Peter Gordon should get a mention – I understand there is a good reason for it this time, but I can't remember what that is. Thanks also to David Rose of the *Surrey Advertiser* for providing some research material from the archive.

I must also thank the team of Paul Ryan (business management), Paul March at Clintons (the lawyers) and Dennis Hill and Olivia Hill (accountants), Margot Weale at Midas Public Relations, Andy Ellis (website editor), Tim Gall at Lloyds TSB and Robert Smith (literary agent).

Finally, a big thanks to all the loyal readers of *Shaggy Dogs and Black Sheep* who have not been conned by spoiler books and imitations this year and who still email the website in vast numbers with ideas and suggestions. Sorry I haven't been able to reply to these: I've been busy working on this latest collection and I hope you'll agree it has been worthwhile.

Introduction

The subject of urban myths and legends is one I have been interested in for a couple of years now. It occurred to me, one day at lunch with friends on the Isle of Dogs, that most long rambling conversations (and ours are certainly long and always rambling) will include a tall tale or two. Someone will then be reminded of a story he or she once heard, which is then presented as near or actual fact. The tale will be introduced like this: 'That reminds me of a story I once heard . . .' or 'I remember my uncle/aunt/sister/hairdresser telling me what happened to a friend of theirs . . .'

So urban legends are easy to spot and always have a ring of truth about them. The events they describe could happen or might have happened to any of us. Each of us could have been as unfortunate or stupid as the character(s) in the story, and that is one of the reasons we all enjoy urban legends so much: that the misfortune involved didn't happen to us but to somebody else. And that makes us laugh. The stories come in many different forms. Some involve ghostly goings-on, some are about love lost or found. Some centre on plain stupidity and some on unfortunate coincidences, although some do have happy endings. The connecting feature is that all are told and then retold and come back around in altered forms, and all of them are passed around by word of mouth or, especially these days, via the internet where they spread like wildfire. These 'legends' (so called 'urban', although they don't need to have an urban setting) are the modern-day version of medieval folklore, and all of the anecdotes in this collection can be recounted the next time you are at lunch or dinner or in the pub with friends. They can make even the most unimaginative person seem interesting, I promise. They seem to be working for me, at any rate.

The research for this book has been fascinating: it was amazing to discover that Winston Churchill really was a Druid or that one Japanese soldier had continued fighting the Second World War on his own for thirty years. But I should point out here that many of the tales told in this collection are probably not true and that any names given, apart from when they are used to back up evidence in genuine accounts, are made up, by me. So, for example, if there really is a Peter Patsalides who worked at the World Trade Center in New York prior to 11 September 2001 (see 'Caught with His Trousers Down'), then I am not suggesting he was having an affair because that is also the name of the friend who told me the story in the first place. So please don't sue if your marriage collapses as a result of something I have written. I am sure many of the stories included must be untrue, but that is part of the fun of urban legends: it is up to us to decide for ourselves what to believe and what not.

As for the title ... What happened was that when Georgina Laycock, my editor at Penguin, returned my first draft with 'THAT'S BOL-LOCKS!' sternly scrawled in red across the top, I naturally assumed that it was her suggested title, as it's such a common reaction to hearing one of these stories. At least, from my friends. It was only after I'd talked everything through with the Penguin (fans of the cult film *The Blues Brothers* will understand why I call her that) that we realized it really was the best title. You need to approach these kinds of stories with a bit of healthy cynicism (well, at least I do) and then it's all the better when, sometimes against all the odds, they turn out to be true. And besides, 'That's bollocks!' is one of my favourite expressions. But we also agreed that the Penguin would have to come down to Guildford and explain to the Women's Institute (and to my mother) what bollocks are – although, at the time of writing, they are still waiting.

Some well-known urban legends are bound to be missing from this book – but they may well pop up in a second volume if this one does well.

(Do drop me a line if you know a really good one I haven't covered, to *info@albertjack.com*.) That would also give me the opportunity to use the title 'Even More Bollocks' and to annoy my mum again – although I promise to grow up soon. It is only meant to be a little bit of fun and perhaps to provoke some thought and conversation. Anything that does that must be a good thing. Besides, reading this book and spreading a few of the tales might make you more popular – you never know.

Finally, I hope you enjoy these stories and then take good care of the book. Now that Georgina has found out she is listed as 'the Penguin' in my phone book, there may not be another one.

Albert Jack
Guildford
May 2006

REVENGE IS A DISH BEST SERVED COLD

The Seafood Effect

June was not a happy lady. Just before Christmas in 1998, her husband Mike left her to start a new life with her closest friend. Having spent the whole winter on her own, June received a letter from a divorce lawyer, asking for possession of the house so that Mike and her old friend could move in. That was when she planned her revenge. She replied to the letter, offering vacant possession on condition the house was sold and the proceeds split between her and Mike. The evening before she was due to move out, June invited her real friends around for a lavish 'Last Supper'. The following afternoon, after the removal men had left, she carefully unscrewed the ends of the metal curtain poles in all the rooms and filled the cavities with spoonfuls of caviar and half-eaten prawns, along with the shells, after which she picked up the rest of her belongings and left the home she loved.

A few weeks later, Mike and his new lady

noticed a lingering smell that became worse as the days passed. They paid to have the house professionally cleaned from top to bottom, the air vents and floorboards checked for dead rats and air purifiers installed in every room, but still the smell grew worse. Before long, the workmen looking for the source of the stench were refusing to enter the house and, as potential buyers were failing to make it past the front door before they fled, the estate agent suggested taking the property off the market until the cause of the smell had been located.

Eventually the couple had to retreat to a hotel before taking out a huge loan and buying another house. Soon afterwards, as chance would have it, June phoned Mike to inquire how the house sale was progressing and listened as her ex-husband made up a story about the depressed housing market and how he had been unable to find a buyer. He was amazed when his former wife offered to buy his share, for a substantially reduced amount. Seizing the chance to burden his ex with the mysteriously smelling property, he accepted a nominal payment for his half share, but not without one last act of meanness. On the day of the transfer, June pulled up with her removal men just in time to find Mike's team stripping the house of all the fixtures and fittings for installation in his new home – shelving, carpets and curtains, right down to door knobs, light bulbs and . . . curtain poles. June's plan had worked to perfection.

In a similarly vengeful vein are the farmer who covered his local bank in slurry in response to needless bank charges, the wife of a cheat who cut one leg off all his trousers before delivering his prized, and expensive, vintage wine collection to the doorsteps of every house in their village with a note explaining his behaviour, and the jilted girlfriend who placed adverts of her former lover in a gay magazine before sending his new partner a copy. We have seen watercress scattered all over an apartment and the heating turned to full while an ex-lover was on holiday and a condom-wearing cucumber strategically left in a place it would easily be found. In fact there are so many such tales of revenge they could fill a book of their own.

The Better Man

There was a huge wedding with about three hundred guests. During the reception the groom stood up to deliver his speech. He said that he wanted to thank everyone for coming, many from far afield, to support him and his new bride on their big day. He especially wanted to thank the bride's family for all attending. The groom then announced that each guest would find, taped to the bottom of his or her chair, a manila envelope. He explained that the envelopes contained his gift to everyone, to convey the strength of his feelings on this occasion, and invited the guests to open them.

Inside each envelope was an 8 × 10 picture of his bride giving the best man oral sex in the latter's back garden. (He had become suspicious and hired a private detective to follow his wife-to-be.) As the wedding guests gasped in shock, the groom turned to his new bride and announced he was leaving her. The marriage was annulled the following day.

Revenge is a Cheap Jaguar

Early one morning, a teenage garage mechanic in Oxford was looking through his local paper for a cheap second-hand car when his attention was caught by one rather puzzling small advert: 'Jaguar XK8 for sale, 2 years old, perfect condition, leather interior and sat. nav. – only £200.' Believing the price to be a misprint that should have read £20,000 at the very least, he moved on to other adverts, but his attention kept drifting back to the one for the Jaguar until he finally made up his mind to telephone the number provided. A well-spoken lady answered and confirmed he was the first caller and that the car was indeed only £200.

Still puzzled, the young mechanic drove to the address given by the lady and found himself at a large country house with landscaped gardens, tennis courts and a swimming pool. Outside the garage was a shiny black Jaguar XK8 being polished by the gardener. The V8 engine purred when the mechanic took it out for a spin and the car was in mint condition, so on checking the price again the mechanic quickly handed over £200 and promptly received the keys and log book in return. He could scarcely believe his luck but had to ask, 'Why are you selling the car so cheaply? Surely you must know it is worth much more?' The lady hesitated and then decided no harm could be done if she explained the story behind it all.

'A few years ago,' she told him, 'I met the perfect man. He was tall, attractive and owned a very successful publishing business. We got married, moved into this house and everything was perfect for three years. Then he employed a beautiful, sexy young PR executive and before I knew it they were having an affair. I found out about a month ago and when I confronted him he admitted everything, packed his bags and left, just like that. Then, last week, I received a letter from his lawyer stating that as long as he could retain my share of the business as well as his own, he was happy for me to keep the house and the rest of the money. But there was one condition: as he didn't want to come back to the house and face me, I was told I had to sell his Jaguar, keep half the money and forward the balance on to him to use as a deposit for a new car. So that is exactly what I am doing.'

Unexpected Reversal

In Weybridge, Surrey, an elegant lady was patiently waiting for a parking space at the shopping centre near the old Brooklands racetrack. After a short while, she noticed a man walking to his car and so she drove closer in order to use the space once he had vacated it. But just as he left, an arrogant youngster nipped past her and forced his boy-racer Escort into the empty bay ahead of her. The lady wound her window down. 'Young man,' she said. 'I have been waiting for that space.'

'Sorry, old girl,' came the reply, 'but that's what happens when you are young and quick.' With that, the lady positioned her Mercedes directly in front of his car and then reversed as fast as she could, smashing the tow bar straight into the Escort, destroying the radiator and the entire front end. As his car sat hissing and leaking water all over the parking bay, the youngster looked on in shocked disbelief. 'You can't do that,' he stammered. 'Yes, you can,' replied the lady. 'You can when you are old and rich.'

We have all, at times, wished we could have delivered a withering put-down in response to an insult. A past master at it was Sir Winston Churchill, who once silenced Lady Nancy Astor after she had fired the barb: 'Winston, if I were your wife I would put poison in your coffee.' The great man shot back: 'Nancy, if you were my wife, I would surely drink it.' On another occasion he was insulted by a young woman who said, 'Mr Churchill, there are two things I don't like about you. Your politics and your moustache.' To which he replied, 'Fear not, madam, for you are not likely to come into contact with either.'

Supermodels can apparently produce wit from

time to time. The following exchange between two of them, who I have decided should remain nameless for the sake of my future health and wellbeing, took place on an international flight. 'I liked your recent autobiography. Who wrote it for you?' 'That's kind of you to say. Who read it to you?' Touché ... (or perhaps 'touchy' is the correct word).

Hunters' Revenge

Three friends were out for a weekend's hunting and they stopped at a remote farm, where one of the men got out to ask the farmer's permission to hunt on his land. The farmer happily granted permission, asking that the man first shoot the old bull in the top field as he had been planning to get rid of it. The hunter went back to the car and decided to play a trick on his friends. He told them the farmer had angrily denied them permission so they must set off to find another location. As they passed the top field, the hunter spotted the bull. With that he stopped his car, pulled out his rifle and shot the bull dead. 'That will teach the miserable old sod a lesson!' he exclaimed. At this, his friends also pulled out their rifles, and before he could stop them they had shot three of the cows dead as well. 'That will really teach him a lesson,' they said.

Dearly Departed

Many people have been tempted to have cryptic messages carved on to either their own headstones or those of loved ones. Spike Milligan famously requested the line in his native Gaelic: 'Duirt me leat go raibh me breoite.' In English this becomes: 'I told you I was ill.' His headstone was finally erected in 2004 at St Thomas's Church in Winchelsea, East Sussex, and the words are a typical example of the great man's humour. Some messages, however, are not so funny and while graveyard owners or the Church usually forbid acrimonious lines on headstones,

Here Lies Buried

John Laird McCaffery

Free Your Body And Soul
Unfold Your Powerful Wings
Climb Up The Highest Mountains
Kick Your Feet Up In The Air

You May Now Live Forever
Or Return To This Earth
Unless You Feel Good Where You Are

there are ways of overcoming the rules. This was so in the case of John Laird McCaffery, who died on 14 August 1995. The stonemason carving the inscription claims he did not notice the hidden message when the deceased man's wife and mistress placed the order for the stone together (see the illustration). They claimed the meaning of the poem was just a personal matter between the three of them.

Reading the first letter of each line vertically will reveal the true message to poor old John. The offending headstone can be found at Section C, Plot 01369 of Montreal's Cimetière Notre-Dame-des-Neiges.

Other famously funny epitaphs include:

Sir Winston Churchill: 'I am ready to meet my Maker. Whether my Maker is prepared for the great ordeal of meeting me is another matter.'

John Brown, dentist: 'Stranger approach this spot with gravity, for John Brown is filling his last cavity.'

The Guildford Gypsies

The A3 is a major and historic road in the south of England, linking London to Portsmouth, the traditional home of the British navy. For centuries, travellers have used the route, which has

been consistently modified, updated, altered and improved. As the modern road passes Guildford and climbs the Hog's Back, you reach the ancient gypsy site that engineers bulldozed through in a road-modifying scheme to include a bridge that would filter traffic away from the A3 and along the Hog's Back towards Farnham. Work began in 1973 and technical problems delayed the opening by a full year. Only months after the bridge finally did open, in 1976, freak rainstorms wrecked the drainage and the road was promptly closed again. This was when the legend of the gypsy curse began circulating, locals believing the bridge would never be safe. An anonymous letter to *The Times* warned: 'They are wasting rate payers' money if they try and shore up the bridge over the A3 because that bridge has a gypsy curse on it.'

Guildford reporter Jane Garrett investigated in 1980 and was told by gypsy community leader Jasper Smith how his grandmother had often recounted stories of the gypsy curse condemning the Guildford end of the Hog's Back. He claimed nothing engineers could do would ever resolve the continuing problems with the roadworks. 'After five years or so, it will go wrong again,' he warned. 'Apparently there was a lot of trouble with the police here many years ago,' he continued. 'Some of the gypsies were prosecuted and sent to prison for camping there illegally.' Locals confirmed to me after a radio phone-in programme that a gypsy camp did once occupy that area and everyone had been evicted to make way for a road-widening scheme. It is believed that the curse was placed on the land at the time of the evictions.

After the bridge was closed in 1976, it in fact reopened again in 1979. It was closed again that year until 1982 for major repairs, then closed again in 1986, 1992 and 1994 for further repair work. Many locals believe in the gypsy curse and have refused to travel over or under the bridge, fearing that it may explode one day. The curse, rather than a series of complicated junctions, is also blamed for many of the accidents that occur at the Guildford end of the Hog's Back.

TALL TALES OF THE RICH AND FAMOUS

Casino Fright

An attractive young lady was on a business trip to Las Vegas. Finding herself alone on her final evening, she decided to go and try her luck in the hotel casino. She had already been warned by colleagues that if she got lucky and had a big win, she should not return to her room alone, but instead call security to escort her back. As luck would have it, the young lady did indeed have a big win, but then was immediately worried about having such a large amount of cash on her person. She decided to go back to her room and place it in the safe and so, following her colleagues' advice, she telephoned the security office.

Unfortunately the guards told her they would not be available for about half an hour and asked her to wait in the reception area. Instead, feeling vulnerable, she decided to take the first lift available and get to her room as quickly as possible. She was relieved to find the first lift empty and stepped in, but, just as the doors were closing, a hand forced itself in and pushed the doors back open.

In walked two large black men wearing hats and dark glasses. One of them growled, 'Hit the floor!' so she did, and cowered in the corner of the lift, quaking with fear. The two men collapsed with laughter and one of them helped her up, explaining he meant the button to his floor. Still shaking violently, the lady explained what she had been told, and about her win, so the two men offered to see her to her room. She politely refused but they insisted, almost frogmarching her along the corridor. Her fears renewed, she was, once again, terrified of being robbed, or even murdered, but instead they gently opened the door, escorted her safely inside and then left.

The following morning, the lady discovered her room bill had already been paid but the receptionist refused to tell her by whom. On her return home, twenty-one bouquets of flowers were delivered to her door. Obviously puzzled, and still a little dazed, she picked up a card attached to one of the bouquets, which read: 'Thank you for the funniest thing that has ever happened to us', signed 'Eddie Murphy and Arsenio Hall'.

It is a wonderful, classic story – if only it were true?

Charlie Chaplin

Star of the silver screen Charlie Chaplin was recognizable throughout the world for his baggy trousers, comedy walk and hilarious antics. Unsurprisingly, Chaplin look-a-like competitions were a regular feature at shows and fairs throughout America in the 1920s and 1930s (rising young star Bob Hope was once a winner himself), and locals had a great time imitating the lovable tramp. Legend has it that Chaplin himself entered one such show in a San Francisco

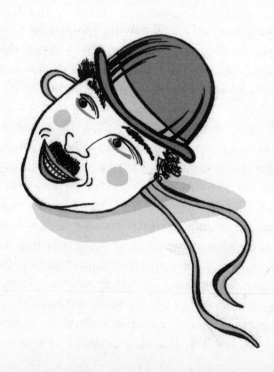

theatre for a bet, telling friends he was 'tempted to give lessons in the Chaplin walk' not only out of pity for the other contestants, but also from a 'desire to see it done properly'.

Certain he would win, Chaplin performed outrageously on stage, expecting his celebrity to be unmasked at any moment. Instead, however, the great man failed even to make the final stages of the competition and the story goes that his brother Syd was the eventual winner.

Star Heckler

A story has circulated among music fans since the early 1970s of a rock concert performed by the American band Grand Funk Railroad during which, after a featured guitar solo, a member of the audience started booing loudly. This was ignored for a short while until a member of the group finally took the microphone and announced, 'The punk booing in the front row, if you think you can do any better, come up and show us!' The crowd was stunned to see Eric Clapton leave his seat and join the band on stage. This story has been repeated and believed for over thirty years, and may in fact be true. But it is hard to imagine that Clapton, respectful as he is of other musicians, would ever have jeered another guitarist. Unless, of course, it was all pre-arranged and the band had already invited Clapton to play. That would make an even better story.

There are several similar tales of famous and talented people not being recognized and being asked to do something at which they excel. For instance, there was a story doing the rounds in the northeast of England during the 1980s of a group of young men challenging another group to a race along the seafront at Newcastle, after an evening's drinking in the town. The second group readily accepted the challenge and put forward their best runner, who just happened to be the reigning Olympic champion and world record holder for running the mile, Steve Cram.

The world of comedy has its own stories too. One such tale is told by the victim himself, one of the many little-known comedians on the US circuit. He claims that one night he was delivering his usual routine, when someone in the audience started heckling him. He traded some banter with the stranger but, running out of witty retorts, had to resort to the old fallback response: 'Hey, you think you can do better?' Apparently the heckler turned out to be none other than master of razor-sharp repartee Robin Williams.

Another tells the story of American comedian Bill Cosby, although sometimes Groucho Marx is the subject. One Sunday morning, the comedian is mowing the grass outside his large house on a wealthy private residential estate. A neighbour passes by and, believing him to be the gardener, asks how much the lady of the house pays him for mowing the lawn. 'Nothing,' comes the reply, 'but she does let me sleep with her every night.'

Celebrity Abuse

A businessman claims he was in the VIP lounge at Heathrow airport waiting for an important customer to arrive when he noticed American billionaire Bill Gates sitting at a nearby table. The businessman says he introduced himself to Gates and asked him if he would come over and say hello to him when his client arrived as he was trying to impress her. Gates agreed and half an hour later, when the client had arrived, he wandered over to the businessman's table and greeted him with the words, 'Hey, Chris, good to see you again. What's happening?' To which Chris replied, 'Not now, Gates – I'm in a meeting.'

If true, this was an appalling thing to do and especially to boast about afterwards. Fortunately, it seems the author of the tale has all the imagination we would expect of him, because he has pinched somebody else's story. The legend can be told about any celebrity and has had a few outings over the years, but the earliest example I can find dates from the 1960s when a story was told about a student who recognized

Frank Sinatra at a nearby table in a restaurant. Wanting to impress his new girlfriend, he introduced himself to the singer and asked him if he would mind pretending to know him. Sinatra agreed and said, 'Hi, Bernie,' as he passed the student's table. The lad then snapped, 'Do you mind, Frank. Can't you see I'm busy?'

Moon the Loon

Keith Moon, late drummer of The Who, died in 1978 and left behind a string of urban legends as a result of his erratic and often comical behaviour. Probably under the influence of drugs, Moon is said to have blown up his drum kit on stage, allegedly damaging guitarist Pete Townsend's hearing in the process. He then befriended a tramp in Soho, after the concert, before checking him into London's Hilton Hotel and continuing to drink with him until the early hours. Moon apparently then forgot all about the tramp, until the hotel phoned his record company over two weeks later to ask what they were supposed to do with the old man and who was paying the bill. The record company dutifully picked up the tab.

Despite being regarded by many as the finest drummer of his generation, Moon's good-natured disruptions led to his band mates barring him from the studio when the vocal parts were being recorded. It has been said that at the end of the recording of 'Happy Jack' Pete Townsend can be heard in the background shouting 'I see ya!' as he spots Moon sneaking into the studio to let off fireworks. Whether any of these tales are true or not, only those close to the band would know. What could be regarded as the most famous rock urban legend of all time is definitely not true, however. According to Steve Grantley (co-author with Alan Parker of *The Who by Numbers*), Keith Moon definitely did not drive his Rolls-Royce into the swimming pool either at his home, as is sometimes suggested, or at the Holiday Inn in Flint, Michigan, where it is also reported to have happened during the drummer's twenty-first birthday party. 'What he did do, though,' says Grantley, 'is reverse it by accident into his garden pond, full of mud and sludge, one morning and then had to ask the AA to tow it back out for him.'

This would come as a surprise to Oasis, however, the English band that perpetuated the myth by featuring a photograph of a Rolls-Royce submerged in a pool on the front of their 1997 album *Be Here Now*. In a similar nod to the legend, *Top Gear* television presenter Jeremy Clarkson opened his local swimming pool at Chipping Norton in June 2005 by driving a Rolls-Royce Silver Shadow into the water as part of a TV escapade organized by the James Bond stunt team Bickers.

Another rock and roll legend tells of Peter Grant, charismatic manager of Led Zeppelin, checking out of a hotel in America one day, peeling off $100 bills from a huge roll of cash to pay for the damage his band and entourage had caused during their stay. Nervously, the hotel receptionist asked, 'Excuse me, Mr Grant, but what is it like to actually throw a television out of the window?' Grant looked down at the lad and after a short pause peeled off another $300, with the words: 'Here you are, son, have one on us.'

Winston Churchill was a Druid

When the Roman army reached the shores of Britain in AD 43, they encountered what appeared to be an uncultured race of people with few skills, little intellect and virtually no compassion – such as can be found on the average Friday night in any suburban town nearly two thousand years later. The Romans swept away Celtic rule in both Britain and Gaul, which was largely held by the Druids, who wielded absolute power as soothsayers, mystics, scholars and, ultimately, judges. It was the Druids who decided whether criminals were innocent or guilty, tying up the accused and throwing them into a river to observe whether they sank or floated, or making them walk through fire to see if the gods

protected them from being burnt. It was also the Druids who decided who would be sacrificed to appease the gods and, as their belief was that the sun would fail to rise without an offering to the sun god, human sacrifices were performed on a regular basis throughout the land. The Romans

knew otherwise, however, and soon put a stop to
this practice. Julius Caesar himself wrote of the
Celts:

All the people of Gaul are completely devoted to
religion, and for this reason those who are greatly
affected by disease and in the dangers of battle either
sacrifice human victims or vow to do so using the
Druids as administrators to these sacrifices, since it
is judged that unless for a man's life a man's life is
given back, the will of the immortal gods cannot be
placated. In public affairs they have instituted the
same kind of sacrifice. Others have effigies of great
size interwoven with twigs, the limbs of which are
filled up with living people, which are set on fire from
below, and the people are deprived of life surrounded
by flames. It is judged that the punishment of those
who participated in theft or brigandage or other
crimes are more pleasing to the immortal gods; but
when the supplies of this kind fail, they even go so low
as to inflict punishment on the innocent.

(From *The Celtic Heroic Age*, edited by John T.
Koch with John Carey, 1995)

The Druids were slaughtered by the Romans,
although they lived on in memory throughout
the Middle Ages. However, the Ancient Order of
Druids was re-established in London in 1781 –
happily excluding human sacrifice – as the new
fashion of belonging to secret societies swept
through English society. Several branches of the

new Druid movement sprang up in Britain, Europe and America with many of them emphasizing the advancement of social ideas, science and the arts while also guaranteeing members' financial assistance in times of business failure or other trouble. Like all good secret societies, they knew when to close ranks.

Given the non-political nature of the modern Druid movement, it is therefore a surprise to find one of history's best-known politicians, Sir Winston Churchill, was himself a Druid. He was also a Mason: his father, Randolph, another prominent British statesman, had been a leading member of the Freemasons, and Winston joined the society after his father's death in 1895, later rising to become Master Mason in 1902, a position he held until he left the Freemasons in 1912.

According to papers held by the Chartwell Trust at Churchill College, Cambridge, Winston joined the Albion Lodge of the Ancient Order of Druids, known as Lodge 59, at a specially convened meeting held at the Wheatsheaf Hotel, High Street, Oxford, on 10 August 1908, the day before he famously proposed to his beloved Clementine in the grounds of nearby Blenheim Palace, his ancestral home. His Druid membership, costing ten shillings and ninepence, was proposed by A. E. Turner and seconded by the Duke of Marlborough, according Churchill the proud status of 'Number 3095 of 59 Lodge in Albion'. Remarkable, given that his occupation at the time was listed as the rather more mundane 'President of the Board of Trade'.

Churchill's association with the ancient order was an open secret at the time, and the young politician is even shown in a photograph in Stuart Piggott's book *The Druids*, standing with a group of men clad in traditional Druid robes, although their newest recruit wears only a morning suit.

By this time, Churchill had been a Member of Parliament for eight years and only two years later was promoted to the position of home secretary, embarking on what would become a journey to the very top, including two periods as British prime minister, the first during the Second World War. As a result, it would appear Churchill had little time for Druid activity and there is no record of him ever attending either the summer solstice at Stonehenge or the winter solstice at the Rollright Stones in Oxfordshire, dressed in robes or otherwise. Neither is there any record of him ever leaving the Ancient Order of Druids, although there is evidence of his lasting beliefs.

The first piece of evidence concerns Churchill's two-fingered 'V for Victory' salute, famously delivered during the Second World War. Some people regard this as a Druid sign demonstrating the hidden 2+3 within the Law of Fives – two fingers up and three bent down signalling 2+3 (two plus three equalling five). (The Law of Fives states simply that all things happen in fives, or are divisible by or multiples of five, or are somehow directly or indirectly related to five.) Others see no such symbolism in the gesture.

Secondly, Churchill is known to have looked into astrology and the occult during the Second World War and had close links with leading occultist Aleister Crowley, once described as 'the wickedest man in the world' and, by his own mother, 'the Beast'. Crowley is credited with creating Churchill's 'V for Victory' sign and popularizing it among Satanists.

The final piece of evidence concerns Churchill's remark that wherever he went in the world he always made sure he was within reach of a piece of wood, which ties in with the ancient Druid belief that all the good and protective spirits in the world live inside trees. Those in distress or in need of good fortune would make their way to the spiritual tree to touch and hug it in search of peace and prosperity.

So there you have it: Sir Winston Churchill, our most famous prime minister and voted in a national BBC poll as the greatest Briton of all time, a fully paid-up and practising member of the Ancient Order of Druids, albeit long after they ceased to practice human sacrifice.

What Goes Around Comes Around

Farmer Fleming was a poor Scottish crofter, working the land to provide his young family with food and clothing, but dreaming of providing them with a better future and a better life than he himself had endured. One morning, the farmer heard cries for help coming from a nearby field and, dropping his tools, he ran in the direction of the voice. There, trapped waist deep in a murky Scottish bog, was a terrified boy steadily sinking into the mud. Disregarding his own safety, Fleming flung himself on the ground by the bog and pulled the boy to safety, saving him from certain death.

The following day, a grand carriage drew up at the modest croft cottage and a noble lord stepped out to greet the farmer. Introducing himself as the father of the boy Fleming had saved, he insisted he wished to reward the farmer to show his gratitude. But Fleming refused, declaring he had acted only as anyone else would have done in the circumstances. At that point, the farmer's own son joined his father. 'Is this your boy?' asked the nobleman, and Fleming proudly agreed that it was. 'In which case I will make you a promise,' said his lordship. 'I will take the boy and pay for the best education money can buy. If he is anything like his father, he will grow into a man we will both be proud of.'

Seeing a chance for his son to escape a life of poverty, the farmer agreed and the boy then benefited from the finest education, finally graduating from St Mary's Hospital medical school in London. He was later knighted for his contribution to medicine and became known as Sir Alexander Fleming, the man who discovered penicillin. Some years later, the nobleman's son became ill with pneumonia and it was penicillin that saved his life, truly repaying the nobleman – Lord Randolph Churchill – for his benevolence. His son, the boy dragged from the bog, was of course none other than Sir Winston Churchill, Britain's celebrated wartime prime minister.

This tale has been circulating for many years, but unfortunately it seems Fleming himself dismissed the story. In Kevin Brown's *Penicillin Man: Alexander Fleming and the Antibiotic Revolution*, published in 2004, he is quoted describing the story merely as 'a wonderful fable'. While it is recorded that Churchill consulted with Sir Alexander Fleming on 27 June 1946 about a staphylococcal infection, which had apparently resisted treatment by penicillin, there is sadly no record of a young Churchill nearly drowning in Scotland or of Lord Randolph paying for Fleming's education.

Good Samaritan

A black lady was driving along a main freeway in America with her two small children when she ran out of petrol. Stranded at the side of a busy road, she was rescued by a passing motorist who then drove the young family to the nearest petrol station, collected some fuel, drove them back to the car and made sure it started before waving them on their way. The following week a brand new Mercedes-Benz was delivered to the Good Samaritan as a gift with a note of thanks signed by Nat King Cole. The stranded family had been his wife and children. You see, kids – good deeds are sometimes well rewarded.

Hitler's Testicle

This has been the subject of great hilarity since the 1940s – at least it has among schoolboys. And the big question is: did Adolf Hitler have two testicles or only one? This wartime legend appears to have started with a song popularized by British soldiers, then passed down to their children after the war, and consequently there are lots of different versions of it, all sung along to the tune of 'Colonel Bogey'. This is the version I grew up with:

Hitler has only got one ball,
The other is in the Albert Hall.
His mother, the dirty bugger,
Cut it off when he was small.

She tied it up on a conker tree,
The wind came and blew it out to sea.
The fishes took out their dishes
And had scallops and bollocks for tea.

There has been much pondering of the big question for the last fifty years. Indeed during the 1970s, when the Russians finally publicized the results of Hitler's autopsy, it was generally believed that the report had been doctored as a result of the British propaganda song, designed to boost morale within the ranks while humiliating Hitler, a vain and sensitive person, in the hope of sending the madman even madder.

But there are also records proving Hitler was wounded in action during the First World War in 1916, at the Battle of the Somme, and that he suffered an injury to the groin. It is further recorded that shortly afterwards, during an examination for venereal disease, Hitler's company commander noted that the soldier had 'only one testicle'.

So it would appear to be true after all, and many historians now accept the validity of the Red Army's autopsy report, which included the line: 'The left testicle could not be found either in the scrotum or on the spermatic cord inside the inguinal canal, or in the small pelvis.' So I am glad we have cleared that up. Adolf Hitler was monorchid after all, but whether his mother really cut it off and hung it in a horse chestnut tree, we can only speculate. Seems a tad unmaternal though, doesn't it? Which leads neatly on to the next legend . . .

Jack Nicholson's Real Mother

Jack Nicholson has been a film star since 1958. In 1975, by the time he was thirty-seven years old, he had starred in over thirty movies, including major hits like *Chinatown*, *Tommy* and *One Flew Over the Cuckoo's Nest*, and had become established as one of the world's leading film actors. But one rumour, or legend, kept circulating until the great man heard it for himself and tried to find out if it was true. The story was that the woman Nicholson had grown up believing was his elder sister was in fact his mother.

In 1975, a reporter from *Time* magazine phoned Nicholson to check the facts of a story that had surfaced about a man claiming to be his father who was alive and well and living in Ocean Grove, New Jersey. The man stated that the woman Nicholson called 'Sis' was in fact his mother and the lady he called 'Ma' was his maternal grandmother. As both women had died many years before, Jack had to verify the truth of the story with his other sister, Lorraine, only to find out she was his aunt after all. The legend had been true. Jack had been born on 22 April 1937 as the illegitimate son of the seventeen-year-old June Nicholson. Her mother, Ethel May, immediately claimed Jack was her own and the women took the secret to their graves. Nobody was ever told and Nicholson himself only found out a decade after his mother had died. His reaction was one of total shock. When asked about it by a reporter working for the *Glasgow Herald*, Nicholson replied, 'It was in 1975 and long after June had died. I was making *The Fortune* for Mike Nichols and somebody called me on the phone to tell me. Ultimately I got the official version from June's sister, Lorraine. I was stunned.'

Einstein's Brilliant Chauffeur

Soon after Albert Einstein had produced his theory of relativity, he set about a university tour of lectures from coast to coast in America. Students flocked to see the scientist with the rapidly growing reputation, and lecture halls were filled to the rafters each time Einstein appeared. Among the audience was his faithful chauffeur Harry, who attended every lecture and once proudly announced to Einstein that he had learned all his employer's presentations off by heart. As the two had become great friends, Einstein suggested they exchange places for one lecture so that Harry could prove this. (At that time, Einstein wasn't the easily recognizable figure he would become.) Einstein would drive Harry to Dartmouth College in New Hampshire and the driver would present his lecture. Harry performed brilliantly and delivered Einstein's lecture word for word while the great man sat in the back row wearing a chauffeur's uniform and pretending to doze off. But disaster was about to strike. As Harry was leaving the speaker's platform, to great applause, one of the college officials asked him a complex question on the theory of relativity, one no doubt involving many detailed calculations and complex equations in response. Harry listened carefully and thought about his reply before announcing: 'The answer to this is simple, in fact it is so simple I am going to let my driver answer it for you.' The fast-thinking chauffeur then left the hall, leaving Einstein to deal with the officials.

Ice Cream Superstar

In a London park, a lady was queuing for an ice cream on a hot summer's day when she recognized her favourite actor Paul Newman standing in the queue in front of her. The film legend smiled and said hello but the lady was so star-struck she could only mumble in reply. Newman then bought his ice cream and stood looking across the park. The lady did the same but as she walked past Newman she realized she had her purse in her hand but no ice cream. Thinking she had left it on the ice cream vendor's hatch, she turned back, but Newman gently touched her arm and said: 'It's in your handbag, right where you put it.'

David Bowie and Mick Jagger

For over forty years, rumour and myth have followed two of the world's biggest stars wherever they have gone. But no story has been more often told and more widely believed than that David Bowie and Mick Jagger, front man of one of the world's most celebrated bands, The Rolling Stones, had a gay love affair during the hedonistic 1970s. But it seems that while it is usually treated as urban legend, there is a scrap of truth to be explored if we are going to get to the bottom of it, so to speak. Now, since it is important to be very scrupulous when dealing with such subjects, we should start with the source of the myth, which we can trace to an edition of *The Joan Rivers Show* broadcast on 4 May 1990. This was the year that the former

Mrs Bowie, Angie, had her ten-year gagging order – part of her divorce agreement with David Bowie in 1980 – lifted. Eager to cash in, Angie promised the *Rivers* production team some salacious gossip for the show and that she was ready to 'dish the dirt'. But when the cameras started rolling, she lost her nerve and maintained she had 'never kissed and told'. Off camera, Angie was harshly reprimanded by Rivers for her 'cowardice' and urged to return to the set, which, after rethinking her situation, she agreed to do. Once there, the subject of her former marriage was raised again and Angie made the remark: 'I caught him in bed with men several times. In fact the best time I caught him in bed was with Mick Jagger.'

Fellow guest, the shock jock Howard Stern, never one to miss an opportunity, asked if the two men had their clothes off, and Angie replied, 'They certainly did.' The news that David Bowie, who had been open about his sexuality during the 1970s, had been caught in this situation was no surprise to anybody, but the idea that one of the world's legendary swordsmen, Mick Jagger, might be bisexual made headline news, and stories revealing further evidence to support this sprang up all over the world. David Bowie's lawyer quickly issued a public statement stating that 'the implication that there was ever a gay affair between David Bowie and Mick Jagger is an absolute fabrication' and Jagger himself dismissed the whole thing as 'complete rubbish'. Angie, it would appear, had been trying to generate publicity for a forthcoming book about her life but within a week was backtracking. On 11 May, she appeared on another TV show claiming: 'I certainly didn't catch anyone in the act. All I found were two people sleeping in my bed. They happened to be naked and they happened to be Mick Jagger and David Bowie and it's not a big deal. It doesn't mean necessarily that they had some sort of affair.' Soon afterwards she was dismissing it as 'old news and the men had merely passed out in bed'.

But the urban legend was by now in full swing and, like all such myths, it appeared to be more convincing the more it was told. If we hear the same story four or five times and each time from a different source, then human nature forces us to consider it to be true. It is the old 'no smoke without fire' syndrome. But that doesn't make it true, of course. A few years later in her aforementioned book, *Backstage Passes*, published in 1993, Mrs Bowie criticized the public for assuming something she had never confirmed, although it is clear she had been implying it over the years. In the book, she plays down the event: 'I went and opened the door and they were, indeed, in there together and were both asleep. I asked them if they wanted coffee and they said yes. That was that.' Later in the chapter, she uses the ambiguity factor again by adding: 'the fact that Mick had a perfectly good bed of his own just three hundred yards away from where he was passed out naked with David – it all added up inescapably in my head as well as my gut. I didn't have to look around for open jars of KY Jelly.'

David Bowie, to his credit, made only one jaded remark about his ex-wife's revelations, being reported in *US Magazine* in 1995 as saying, 'About 15 or 16 years ago I really got tired of fending off questions about what I used to do with my penis during the early 1970s. My suggestion for people with prurient interests is to go through the thirty or forty biographies on me and pick the rumour of their choice.'

But, in truth, it seems the relationship between Bowie and Jagger has never been anything more than a friendship, despite the former Mrs Bowie's claim. I, for one, would never judge a man, whoever he is, on the testimony of his ex-wife as that is guaranteed to be unobjective. But the myth raised further questions at the time and fingers were pointed at the Rolling Stones' hit song 'Angie', released in 1973, about an illicit love affair. Angie had assumed it was about her, as did most people. It might have been, but others have concluded it was about David Bowie himself, although it is also claimed that Keith Richards wrote it for Anita Pallenberg and that it has nothing to do with Jagger or the Bowies at all.

Marianne Faithfull's Mars Bar

Jagger has been the subject of other enduring urban legends, the most famous of them being the 'Mars Bar inside Marianne Faithfull' myth, which began to circulate following a drugs raid on Keith Richards' Redlands estate by Sussex police in 1967. After an anonymous tip-off, nineteen officers made a surprise raid on the house in February that year looking for illegal class A drugs and, we are told, were lucky enough to find an orgy in progress. We can imagine the police report: 'I proceeded in a westerly direction into the lounge and found Mr Jagger and the said Miss Faithfull in a compromising position with a well-known item of confectionery. So I said to them, "'Ello, 'ello, 'ello: what's going on 'ere then?"'

At least that was basically the story that emerged, and it has been repeated so many times that many people assume it is true: 'I can believe it – you know what that Jagger's like.' The trouble is, it isn't. Despite the sales of Mars Bars shooting up, presumably to inventive lovers (although my girlfriend always preferred Snickers – she liked the nuts apparently), the police report states that they did not burst into the house to find the mother of all orgies going on, but instead politely knocked on the door and waited for it to be answered by Richards. One of the guests,

Christopher Gibbs, later told reporters the scene was one of 'pure domestic normality'. Marianne Faithfull, in her own autobiography, resisted any Angie Bowie-style sensationalism, dismissing the tale as 'demonization' and a malicious twisting of the facts. She later called the story a 'dirty old man's fantasy and a cop's idea of what people get up to on acid'.

A month later, Richards and Jagger appeared at Chichester magistrates' court charged with drug offences, and much was made of Faithfull's appearance on the afternoon of the raid. She had just had a bath and was dressed in nothing but an orange bathrobe. One police officer testified in court that she had deliberately 'let the robe slip to reveal intimate parts of her body'. He saw this as a clear sign of drug use and Faithfull later admitted she did give the officer a 'quick flash'. All of this was sensational stuff for the press and stories headlined every tabloid newspaper, sowing the seeds of the Mars Bar myth. But although Jagger and Richards did receive prison sentences for possession of drugs, later quashed by the appeal court, the rest of one of rock and roll's most enduring legends is simply untrue. Still, why spoil a good story with facts?

Van Halen and the Brown M&M's

Another popular rock and roll legend assures us that the veteran American glam rock band Van Halen insisted in all of their contracts for live performances that a large bowl of M&M's be provided in the dressing room with all the brown ones removed. And this marvellous piece of *Spinal Tap*-style behaviour turns out to be true, although rumours that the band rioted and smashed up their dressing room when they discovered an offending brown M&M at a venue in New Mexico are unfounded.

During the mid 1970s, venues for rock concerts began to change from the packed sweaty clubs of the 1960s through the larger theatres favoured by bands like The Rolling Stones and The Beatles, to the stadium events and festivals that the supergroups such as Led Zeppelin, Electric Light Orchestra and Lynyrd Skynyrd would perform at. As these global rock bands attracted so many fans, they were not only able to ask promoters for more money but would insist on an ever-growing list of personal demands. Out went the crate of beer and a few clean towels earlier groups could expect in more innocent times, to be replaced by inches-thick contracts of catering and technical requirements for individual shows.

Van Halen was one of the first bands to put on

'supershows' and their requirements were so complicated it took a small army of road crew and technicians to meet them. They would turn up at venues with nine trucks of equipment and a list of intricate demands – from the positioning of lighting rigs and the size of the stage doors, down to where the plug sockets were located on stage and how many were provided – that could determine whether the show went ahead or not. The band developed a clever way of checking if a venue manager or promoter had read their contract properly. Hidden away in the contract, somewhere between the spacing of the onstage plug sockets and the direction of the lighting, would be Clause 126, which read: 'There will be no brown M&M's in the back-stage area, upon pain of forfeiture of the show, with full compensation.' Of course, Van Halen never did cancel a show simply as a result of finding brown M&M's, but as lead singer Dave Lee Roth explained in his autobiography, 'So, when I would walk backstage, if I saw a brown M&M in that bowl ... well, line-check the entire production. Guaranteed you're going to arrive at a technical error. They didn't read the contract. Guaranteed you'd run into a problem. Sometimes it would threaten to just destroy the whole show. Something could be, like, literally, life-threatening.'

So the demand wasn't really a case of rock-star excess or petulance at all, just an effective and simple way to check if the concert promoter had read the contract properly. If certain details haven't been attended to, double-check everything. As far as the riot is concerned, the scene has been exaggerated into rock and roll proportions. At a small university venue where the band was due to be performing, Lee Roth had discovered a makeshift stage on a rubber-based basketball arena. Already suspecting the worst, the singer went straight backstage and found brown M&M's in the bowl provided. Seeing this, he kicked a hole in the door in frustration and then threw the buffet across the floor – not because of the brown M&M's as such, but because they indicated the contract had not been read properly and the show might have to be cancelled. The press, however, took the story at face value and reported how Van Halen had caused $85,000 worth of damage in a mini riot after discovering the 'wrong-coloured sweets' in their dressing room.

Princess Diana – The Truth

Whenever famous people die suddenly, especially in the case of Princess Diana, nobody can ever accept it as an accident or nature taking its course. It is equally true of James Dean, Elvis, Buddy Holly, President Kennedy, Marilyn Monroe and many more. Her death spawned so many urban legends and conspiracy theories that it would be a mistake not to cover Princess Diana in these pages.

Oh, I can't be bothered after all. Haven't we all heard enough about this now?

NOT SUCH A GOOD IDEA

Japanese Suicide

A Japanese man had decided to end it all by gassing himself in his oven, but he failed to seal the doors and windows properly. Unfortunately, a passing neighbour lit a cigarette in the hallway outside the man's apartment and a huge explosion destroyed the block of flats they were living in, killing twelve other residents in the process. But the suicidal man survived thanks to his oven, which shielded him as the building fell down around him. He was later convicted on twelve counts of manslaughter and sentenced to life imprisonment in jail where, presumably, he wasn't allowed anywhere near the kitchens.

Caught in the Headlights

Travelling along a road crossing the Pennines, three young motorcyclists were riding back from a party late at night. At one point, the lead rider looked behind him to find his companions weren't on his tail but he could see their headlights about a mile behind him. The road was deserted, so he decided to play a trick on his friends by turning off his lights. When they passed him, side by side, he planned to ride between them and give the boys a fright. As they approached, he lined himself up between their headlights and accelerated towards them. He realized the two headlights were actually those of a delivery van only when it was far too late.

Alive and Buried

A convicted armed criminal had been caught and sentenced to twenty-five years in prison during the 1970s. A short way into his sentence at Strangeways Prison, near Manchester, he found out that whenever a prisoner died, his body would be placed in a coffin in the morgue and nailed shut by the morgue caretaker before being released for burial. One night he hatched a risky plan that would give him the chance of escape. The proceeds from his recent bank raids had remained hidden and the man planned to move to the other side of the world and begin a new life. After befriending the caretaker, he made a deal with him to share his ill-gotten gains if he agreed to nail him into the coffin alongside the next deceased prisoner and then dig him back up after the funeral. The plan worked like a dream and the lag squeezed himself inside the coffin, along with a torch and some food, and settled down to wait for his release. After the funeral service, knowing he would soon be rescued and would have his freedom, he decided to take a look at the prisoner he was temporarily sharing a tomb with. However, using the torch, he discovered his neighbour to be the very caretaker himself, who had died the previous day. And nobody else knew he was down there.

Accident Report

Here is a story that is supposed to come directly from an insurance claim form and has been doing the rounds for about five years. After a serious accident, a man claimed on his insurance policy but the company asked for a detailed explanation of how his injuries had occurred. This was apparently his reply:

I am writing in response to your request for additional information. For section 3 of the accident reporting form I put 'poor planning' as the cause of my accident and you said in your letter that I should explain this in more detail, so I trust the following information will be sufficient.

I am an amateur radio operator, and on the day of the accident I was working alone on the top section of

my new eighty-foot aerial tower. When I had finished building the wall at the top, I discovered that I had, over the course of several trips up the tower, taken up around 300 pounds of tools and bricks that I didn't need. Rather than carry them back down by hand, I decided to lower the items in a wooden barrel by using the pulley attached to the gin pole at the top of the tower. Securing the rope at ground level, I went to the top and loaded everything into the barrel. Then I went back to the ground and untied the rope, holding it tightly to ensure a slow descent of the 300-pound load.

You will note in section 11 of the accident reporting form that I weigh only 155 pounds, somewhat less than the barrel, which came hurtling down, pulling me off my feet. Due to my surprise at being jerked off the ground so suddenly, I lost my presence of mind and forgot to let go of the rope. Needless to say, I proceeded at a rather rapid rate up the side of the tower. In the vicinity of the forty-foot level, I met the barrel on its way down. This explains my fractured skull and broken collarbone. Slowed only slightly by the impact, I continued my rapid ascent, not stopping until the fingers of my right hand were two knuckles deep into the pulley, which accounts for the hand injuries. Fortunately, by this time, I had regained my presence of mind and was able to hold on to the rope in spite of the pain. At approximately the same time, however, the barrel hit the ground, the bottom smashed and everything fell out.

Without the weight of the tools and bricks, the barrel weighs approximately twenty pounds. I refer you again to my weight in section 11. As you might imagine, I consequently began a rapid descent back down the side of the tower. In the vicinity of the forty-foot level, I made contact with the barrel again, which accounts for the two fractured ankles and the lacerations of my legs and lower body. The encounter with the barrel slowed me enough to lessen my injuries when I fell on to the pile of bricks and, fortunately, only three vertebrae were cracked. But I couldn't move, and I am sorry to report that, as I lay there in abject pain and watching the empty barrel eighty feet above me, I once again lost my presence of mind and let go of the rope. I trust this is all the information you need to process my claim.

Whether this insurance claim is a true one or not, I have been unable to establish. It can be traced to Gerard Hoffnung's famous bricklayer story, delivered in a speech to the Oxford Union in 1958, but whether the comic monologue is entirely his own invention or based on an urban legend doing the rounds at the time, we can only speculate. What is certain is that the story circumnavigates the globe via email, purporting to be true.

Stuck to the Van

Possibly inspired by a certain wallpaper-paste commercial, a prisoner in Melbourne, Australia, attempted to escape by gluing himself underneath a laundry van as it left the compound. When the van came to a halt at traffic lights a few miles down the road, he saw his chance to unzip his overalls and slip out to freedom. However, the industrial glue had seeped into the zip and no amount of struggling would free him from his prison uniform. He was eventually re-arrested nine hours later when the van returned to the prison and his cries for help were heard.

The Flying Deckchair

Harry's childhood ambition had been to fly and he studied hard at school to earn the qualifications that would allow him to join the Royal Air Force. He had hoped to become a fighter pilot and was naturally disappointed to find out he couldn't due to his poor eyesight. He soon left the air force and whiled away his days sitting in a deckchair in the garden watching the jets overhead from a nearby airbase. One day, however, Harry had a bright idea: he would fly after all. He made a trip to an army surplus shop and bought forty weather balloons and three helium canisters before returning to his back garden. Harry then secured his deckchair to a nearby tree and began to fasten the balloons to the arms. When he was ready, he took a packed lunch and some cans of beer from the fridge and began to fill the balloons with helium. He was happy to see his plan work when the chair began to lift from the grass and hovered several feet above the ground. Using the air rifle he had brought with him and a can of pellets, he planned to spend the afternoon floating just above roof level firing at birds as they flew past. He also believed he could shoot a few balloons when it was time to land.

However, despite all Harry's careful planning, he would be the first to admit he was no expert when it came to flying. He was somewhat

surprised, therefore, after untying the rope tethering him to the tree, to find himself shooting into the air like a rocket, climbing to a height of 11,000 feet at a speed NASA would have been proud of. Scared witless, he didn't dare shoot any of the balloons in case he unbalanced his makeshift craft and found himself with even more problems, so there he hovered, for fourteen hours. And that's when the real trouble started, as he drifted into the major approach of the nearby airbase runway.

The first pilot to spot him found himself reporting to flight control that a lad in a deckchair with a lunchbox, a pack of beers and a gun was floating at 11,000 feet above the airbase. This caused a major security alert and an RAF helicopter was dispatched to investigate. As darkness fell, Harry found himself being pursued by a military helicopter whose blades were creating enough wind for Harry's deckchair to accelerate to around seventy miles per hour. Eventually the helicopter pilot positioned himself several hundred feet above Harry's 'aircraft' and rescuers were lowered down to attach a safety harness to the young man and winch him up. Back on terra firma, Harry was arrested by military police and when asked what the hell he was doing, replied nonchalantly, 'A man can't just sit around doing nothing all afternoon, can he.'

I would love this story to be true, but somehow I doubt it. Surely it is just an urban legend told and retold until people believe it actually happened.

How to Lose a Light Bulb

A man had replaced the fluorescent light bulb in his kitchen and now had to find a way of disposing of the old one safely. At six feet long the dustmen would not take it and he didn't want to leave it lying around in the garden, so he decided to take it to work and place it in the large bins they had there. However, while he was on the crowded underground, clutching his six-foot white light bulb, two other passengers squeezed in alongside him and also took hold of the light bulb, believing it to be a handrail. The man simply let go and got off at the next stop. It was somebody else's problem now. And maybe a good idea after all?

THE DAILY GRIND

The Case of the Exploding Lighter

In the mid 1970s, a story circulated among workers on a section of railway in the north of England of a man who had his leg blown off by a plastic disposable lighter in his trouser pocket. Apparently he had been welding tracks when a spark seared through his trousers and burned into the lighter, causing an explosion that cost him his leg. A few years later, this story was given sufficient credence that a safety officer at a prominent British airbase began issuing written safety instructions forbidding crewmen from carrying lighters anywhere near an aircraft. However, there is no substantial proof of anybody, engaged in welding or otherwise, having their leg blown off by a cheap plastic lighter.

How to Do It Properly

In American law, companies and corporations are considered to be separate entities from their owner or owners and absurd court cases can arise as a result. One such case involved the owner of a 95 per cent share in a major Californian firm who was injured in an accident at work in 1977. He hired a solicitor to act for him as an employee and a different law firm to act for the company he owned and then worked with both to thrash out a satisfactory settlement for his injury. This clever piece of thinking won him a payout of $122,000, which his company received tax relief on and which he, as the employee, received tax-free. I am now going to spend the afternoon here trying to think of a plausible keyboard injury that I can sue myself for.

Work Till You Drop

George McKline was a hard-working and diligent man. He was employed as a proofreader for a scientific publication in New York and took his work very seriously. As silence was the order of his day, George was allocated a glass-panelled office in the corner of the open-plan floor at the publishing house where he had been a valued

employee for thirty years. He was the first to arrive for work each morning and the last to leave at night, and was held in high regard by all forty-three people working on the same floor as himself.

One morning George's wife turned up at the reception desk in a state of great agitation, claiming her husband had not returned home for three nights and was not answering her calls. Surprised at this, George's boss informed Mrs McKline that her husband was sitting at his desk as normal and offered to accompany her to his office to find out what the problem was. In no time at all, the mystery was unravelled when they discovered George had in fact expired and was propped up in his chair facing away from the rest of his co-workers. An autopsy later confirmed he had died of a heart attack four days earlier, and yet nobody had noticed. According to his boss, Elliot Travers, George was always so absorbed in his work and kept himself so much to himself that nobody ever interrupted him. It was apparently not unusual for him to be seen sitting at his desk in the same position all day long. Ironically George had been proofreading a medical textbook when he died.

Presumably George normally looked dead when he was working as colleagues failed to notice any difference in him. Perhaps all of us should wonder how we appear to colleagues when we are slaving at our desks. I, for example, could probably sit here dead for years before anybody noticed. There is also the tale of a middle-aged woman who was found sitting dead on a tube train travelling London's Circle Line as the train made its last journey of the day. Her friends later confirmed she would have boarded the train at eight o'clock in the morning, on her way to work, and would normally have got off at around 8.30 a.m. Investigators concluded she had travelled around all day and the thousands of fellow passengers who used the same service must have assumed she was only asleep, or perhaps drunk.

Dumb Criminal

In 2003, Richard Schick, formerly employed by the Illinois Department of Public Aid, sued the organization for sexual discrimination and for causing his disability. He claimed $5 million plus an additional $166,700 in unpaid income, and the jury were so sympathetic to his situation that they awarded him the full amount. However, it was also revealed that in the meantime he had become so stressed by the situation he decided to rob a supermarket with a loaded shotgun. The award for compensation was reversed on appeal, although Schick still received $303,830, which he can start spending just as soon as he completes his ten-year sentence for armed robbery.

Nervous Hairdresser

At the end of a long day, a young hairdresser was just about to close her salon when an old man came in for a trim. At first the girl was not too worried about being alone in the salon but her fears rose as she noticed the old chap's hand making a rhythmic up-and-down motion beneath the gown. He gave her a leering, oily smile and the hand movements speeded up. At once, the young hairdresser grabbed a nearby vase and smashed it on the head of the customer before calling the police. When they arrived and examined the scene, officers removed the gown and revealed the man had his glasses in one hand and a duster in the other. He had been cleaning them under the gown while having his hair cut. The unconscious man was taken to hospital and the hairdresser charged with assault.

Quite a Shock

An electrician working for a local council had been asked to replace the bulbs in the streetlights along the high street. Working alone, he was on top of his ladder removing one of the protective lenses when he noticed an irritating stone in his shoe. Rather than take his shoe off, he tried to shake it out. A passing pensioner, out walking his dog, saw the man's leg violently shaking and believed the workman was receiving an electric shock. He rushed over to the rescue and pulled the ladder away, sending the electrician crashing to the ground and breaking both of his legs.

Positive Drugs Test

A croupier at a well-known London casino tested positive for cocaine use and was summarily dismissed from his position. The croupier repeatedly denied the accusation but casino managers felt they had to make an example of him to other staff and refused to accept his plea of innocence. The croupier decided to employ a firm of solicitors to take up his case for unfair dismissal, and investigators insisted all casino staff were tested for cocaine use. Every one of them tested positive and managers were in a state of panic until the truth was revealed. After further tests, the croupier's solicitor was able to prove that all casino staff were innocent of cocaine abuse and that the problem lay with their customers. Most of them were regular cocaine users and the £20 notes they used to buy gambling chips nearly all contained traces of cocaine, which was being transferred to staff as they handled the money, presumably along with all the germs found in most noses.

Jumping Trains

Mr Hobbs had boarded the last train to Doncaster late one Friday evening and was keen to get home for the weekend. However, during the journey he found out from another passenger that the train did not stop at Doncaster and instead travelled all the way to York and there was no return service until the following day. Mr Hobbs had been in this situation before, however, and knowing the train slowed down to almost walking pace at Doncaster station, he decided to take his chances and hop off. As the train pulled into the platform, he opened the door, dropped out his briefcase and overnight bag and jumped off, running alongside the carriage before slowing down. He thought his plan had succeeded to perfection until the following carriage caught up with him and another passenger opened the door and pulled him right back in. 'You were lucky,' said the passenger. 'Didn't you know the train doesn't stop at Doncaster? I saw you running along the platform and thought you were going to miss it.' Mr Hobbs watched his bags disappear into the distance as the train gathered speed.

Life-changing Moments

A country boy who has had little luck in finding a job applies to become the bookkeeper of a London brothel. On his first day, the owners find out he is illiterate and so terminate his employment with immediate effect. But feeling sorry for him, the manager gives the lad three large red apples to take with him. Outside in the street, the boy places the apples on top of a metal dustbin and bends down to tie up his shoelaces when a passer-by offers to buy the apples. The boy then goes off and buys some more apples and soon sells them on for a profit. He does this every day, graduating to a fruit and veg market stall, followed by a shop, a super-market and eventually a national chain of super-markets. Later in life, now a multi-millionaire, he is honoured at a businessman of the year award and a journalist discovers he is still illiter-ate. He asks the businessman what he thought he might have achieved in life if he had been able to read and write, and the man famously replies, 'I would have been the bookkeeper in a Soho brothel.'

Similar tales of 'accidental' success have always been told. Indeed the author W. Somerset Maugham used the same basic plot for his short story 'The Verger' (published in 1929), describ-ing it as a 'well-known bit of Jewish folklore'.

LOVE IS A DANGEROUS BUSINESS

Does It Get Worse Than This?

An unnamed girl – let's call her Jen – was in her first year at college. She was bored and surfing the net one night when she decided to log on to a chat room. There she met a man who identified himself as 'Jeremy'. For safety's sake, she called herself 'Sally' and started describing in detail what she would like to do to him. He responded by telling her to picture his hands running over every inch of her body.

The following evening, they were both back online and becoming more and more intimate, exchanging details about their lives. However, Jen didn't tell Jeremy that she was at college, because she was afraid of sounding immature. This went on for several months and, by the end of the year, they had exchanged the most intimate thoughts and yet had never even spoken on the telephone.

They finally decided they were in love and had to meet. Jeremy told Jen he thought she could be his next wife. Jen was wary at first but decided she didn't care how old he was or how ugly, she had fallen in love with his mind. He was the only man she had ever felt truly comfortable with.

So . . . they planned a weekend together. Jen wanted their first meeting to be private and properly intimate, so she suggested that he book the hotel room and they would meet there, as that way there would be no mistake. Jeremy agreed and booked the hotel. Jen showed up first and checked into the room, where she lit some candles and put on soothing music. She then undressed and lay seductively on the bed, deciding to surprise Jeremy when he came in. Soon she heard a key turn in the lock. A man walked in, and she whispered, 'Jeremy?' He fumbled for the light and turned it on to see Jen lying naked on the bed before him. The next things the hotel manager reported hearing were two loud screams and a mortified girl's voice screeching, 'Dad!'

And let that be a warning to all you inveterate surfers of the net!

Caught Short

This is the fantastic little tale of a young (nameless) man, the son of a wealthy influential London bookmaker. One day his father gave a summer

party at his offices on Piccadilly in the heart of London's West End. The lad, fresh out of college, duly attended prior to a date with his new girlfriend later that evening. A little nervous of both events, our hero spent the first hour at the party mixing whisky and champagne, a calamity in the making. Wet behind the ears and at that time ignorant of the danger of alcohol when consumed in great quantities, the lad was not expecting to lose control of his bowels and soil his trousers before five in the afternoon. In a blind panic, the hapless chap waddled along to Simpson's of Piccadilly and asked the first assistant he saw for a pair of trousers. 'What sort of trousers?' inquired the assistant. 'Any sort at all!' he cried. 'The first pair in my size you can find.' With that he paid for his purchase, grabbed the bag and ran out into the street to hail a cab to take him to the station.

Once safely on the train home, he telephoned his new girlfriend and arranged to meet her at the station, then went along to the lavatory to clean himself up as best he could. Carefully removing his belt and the contents of his pockets, he chucked his dirty trousers and underwear out of the window as the train sped through the countryside. Breathing a long sigh of relief, he then turned to the Simpson's of Piccadilly bag, reached in and drew out – a smart cashmere V-neck sweater. In his haste he had grabbed the wrong bag.

This is where the story ends, but there is more fun to be had with it. For example, we now know he is in the toilet of a fast-moving train, naked from the waist down with little hope of covering his modesty. He could of course squeeze his legs into the arms of the sweater, but which way round does the V go – to the front or to the rear? I suppose he would have to choose his best side and leave that exposed, whichever side he thought that should be. Even then, he has his new lady to confront. Should he get off a stop early or a stop later – and how does he explain not meeting her? Also, what would the ticket collector or other passengers make of him? He is probably a broken man by now and I doubt he drinks much whisky, or champagne. I don't

In Big Trouble Now

When Tony Blair's Labour government replaced
the last Conservative administration in 1997,
many changes were made throughout the Diplomatic Service. One very senior diplomat was
recalled from the British embassy in Thailand.
He informed his wife they would have to be very
careful with their money until such a time as he
received a new posting abroad. His wife then
decided to make an inventory of all the valuable
possessions they had collected during their overseas adventures and auction them to raise some
extra cash.

One of these items was a bronze medallion
she had found while unpacking her husband's
cases a year or two earlier. The diplomat was
at a loss to explain how he had acquired the
medal, so his wife assumed it must have been
one of the many gifts they had received over the
years. There was an inscription engraved on the
back written in Thai, but anybody she asked
was either unable to translate it or simply dismissed it as a maker's stamp. Sotheby's included
the medallion in one of their Eastern collections,
but the diplomat had some explaining to do
when the catalogue arrived at their home. The

description of the medal read: 'Traditional bronze medallion with inscription in Thai reading "Bangkok Prostitute – Authorized Number 441".'

Come Out with Your Hands Up!

Police in Oklahoma had surrounded a house following reports that the occupier had barricaded himself in after an argument with his wife and was both armed and dangerous. A tense stand-off ensued for the following ten hours, and as dusk drew nearer, tear gas canisters were fired in through the windows. At that point the man's wife, apparently unaware of the siege, returned home from work demanding to know what was going on. Police explained about her husband's deranged behaviour, saying that he had refused to communicate with them all day from inside the house. 'That's because he is standing right there,' she replied, pointing to a bystander who had been shouting along with the police all day for the man to give himself up. It turned out nobody was in the house after all and it had been a false alarm. Earlier, however, when the house owner had attempted to identify himself to the police chief, he had been told a dangerous man had barricaded himself inside the house, to stay behind the cordon and let the police do their job. So he did.

Unexpected Inheritance

Two travelling salesmen, one married to the other one's sister, were on a trip to the West Country to attend a sales conference during the 1960s. On arriving in town, they booked into a large, comfortable guesthouse run by an elegant divorcee. After dinner and a few drinks in town, the pair returned to the guesthouse for a nightcap and found the landlady sitting alone in the bar. They joined her for a few more drinks before the single man decided to return to his room to prepare for the following day's work. His sister's husband remained with the landlady and eventually slipped off to her room for a night of illicit passion with her. The following morning, the lady mentioned she didn't know the salesman's name and he, foolishly as it turned out, gave his colleague's name instead of his own. Over the ensuing years, the man regularly made trips to the area, staying in the hotel, using his brother-in-law's name and continuing his affair with the landlady. Then, many years later, the man received a visit one morning from his brother-in-law, who was holding an official-looking letter from a firm of solicitors in the West Country. 'The strangest thing has happened,' he told his sister and her husband. 'Do you remember the hotel we stayed in before the conference all those years ago?' The man froze, as he admitted he did.

'Well, the old lady who owned it has apparently died, and left me the deeds to the hotel and over a million pounds in cash in her will.'

Lottery Prank Backfires

A woman decided to play a practical joke on her husband by pretending he had won the national lottery. With the help of his workmates, she printed an official-looking letter and a friend telephoned him at work, impersonating a lottery official. The confirmation letter was hand-delivered to his office and the man began celebrating his good fortune. A little later, his wife turned up and was puzzled that he had not telephoned her with the news. 'That's because I have been sleeping with your best friend,' he told her. 'Now I am worth five million, I'm leaving you.'

Licensed Prostitute

A businessman had been invited to dinner at the home of his boss and on arriving noticed a framed certificate issued by the police authorities licensing his boss's respectable wife to work as a prostitute in Madagascar. Surprised and a little unnerved, the businessman enjoyed a fabulous meal with the couple, accompanied by fine wine, and as the conversation became more relaxed, the businessman finally found the courage to ask about the certificate. The couple laughed and explained they displayed it as there was a funny story attached. Apparently they had been on holiday in Madagascar when the man had to return to their hotel room after forgetting his wallet. While his wife waited for him, pacing around the hotel lobby, local police arrested her for soliciting sex without the proper authority. Her husband was summoned to the police station and, faced with the choice of paying a large fine for his wife's unlicensed solicitation or the small fee for the prostitute licence, he had chosen the cheaper option. Luckily for him, his wife could see the funny side, which was why the licence was now on display at their home.

Caught with His Trousers Down

A lot of urban legends revolve around being in the wrong place at the wrong time. But what about when you're in the right place at the right time? This applies to no one more than Peter Patsalides, a successful Cypriot businessman. During the afternoon of 10 September 2001, Peter telephoned his wife to let her know about an important business meeting, which had been arranged in his office at the World Trade Center, New York, for the following morning. As urgent preparations needed to be made, he and his colleagues would be working late into the evening. This was not an unusual occurrence, so Mrs Patsalides was untroubled by her husband booking into a hotel for the evening, rather than tackling the hundred-mile commute home.

Peter, however, had other ideas. No meeting was taking place at all and instead our Cypriot hero was off with his 24-year-old secretary a few miles north of the city for, well, some extra dictation. The following morning, when he turned his mobile phone back on, it rang immediately. 'Where are you?' demanded his wife in a frantic and panicked tone. While the rest of the world was watching the North Tower collapse to the ground on live television, Patsalides launched his defence. 'For God's sake, Helen,' he barked. 'What is the matter with you? You know where I am, I'm at the office.'

There were, of course, thousands of people caught up in the catastrophic events of 9/11 who were very much in the wrong place at the wrong time. Then there were those who apparently took advantage of this. Rumour has it that a number of survivors, although no one knows how many, used it as an excuse to walk quietly away from work-related, financial or personal problems, leaving others to assume they had been caught up in the devastation while they began new lives in other parts of the world.

Sex in Costume

After being invited to a fancy-dress Halloween party, Kevin and Katie had both chosen costumes without telling the other what they would be wearing. On the evening of the party, Katie felt unwell and decided not to go, but watched as Kevin dressed up as Spiderman, complete with face mask, and left for a night out. About an hour before midnight, Katie had been feeling better and was bored at home on her own so decided to go to the party after all and surprise Kevin, but when she arrived she found him dancing and flirting with the other guests. Realizing he did not know what her costume was, she decided to put him to the test and see how far he would take his flirting. As the evening wore on, she danced and played with him, eventually leading him outside for sex in the garden. Afterwards she said her goodbyes and returned home, sitting up in bed furiously waiting for her cheating husband to arrive. When he did, she asked him coldly, 'So how was *your* evening?' But Kevin replied, 'Quiet really. I dropped in to your mother and father's house on the way. I didn't particularly feel like going without you, but your dad was really keen, so I lent him my costume and watched television with your mum instead. Apparently he had a great time.'

Ex-boyfriend

Medical students in their final year had not been looking forward to the final autopsy they were expected to attend. But when the day came, they all reluctantly filed into the examination room to be met by their professor, who announced they were lucky to have taken delivery of a recently deceased young man who had tragically taken his own life the previous day. As the professor removed the white sheet, a young female student cried out and ran from the room. It was her ex-boyfriend whom she had not seen since she ended their relationship two days before.

STRANGE BUT TRUE?

Dressing for the Funeral

M. J. Reiderman, a Beverly Hills boutique specializing in expensive ball gowns and evening dresses, used to operate a lenient returns policy, but they have stopped that now. They stopped it after a returned dress was sold on to a wealthy woman who intended to wear it to a large charity gala. During the evening of the gala the woman had broken out in a painful rash and her condition had rapidly deteriorated to the point where an ambulance had to be called and she was rushed to hospital. After a thorough examination, doctors discovered that it was the dress that had made her so ill and she sent her medical invoice to M. J. Reiderman with a threat of legal action.

The shop's owners were forced to act and tracked down the original buyer. A month earlier, the woman's mother had died and her last wish was to be buried in that very dress, which she had long admired in M. J. Reiderman's

window. Unwilling to bury such an expensive item, the woman had retrieved the dress from the undertaker, after the burial service, and returned it to the boutique. It turned out the second buyer had been allergic to the formaldehyde that had soaked into the material. Which just goes to show you that anything we buy could have been returned to the shop after being exposed to all sorts of horrors. It doesn't bear thinking about, does it?

The Harley-Davidson Legend

A New Zealander found himself a summer job on a rural American farm, deep in the country-side. While working there he noticed a rusting

Harley-Davidson motorbike in one of the barns, and the farmer agreed to sell it to him for $5,000. Harley-Davidsons are very popular, but rare in New Zealand, so at the end of his summer shift the lad took the bike home and renovated it carefully. Soon his new bike became the toast of the town and the lad was recognized wherever he went but, wanting to fund a round-the-world trip, he decided to sell it. He was amazed when his first prospective buyer offered him $30,000 on the spot and then the second immediately upped that to $50,000. The lad realized he had no idea how much the bike was worth and telephoned the New Zealand importers of Harley-Davidsons. When he gave them the serial number over the phone, they sent an expert around straightaway who offered him $200,000. Becoming suspicious, he telephoned the company's head office in America, and they flew over one of their representatives who checked the bike and then offered a cool half million! Delighted, he accepted the offer and as the paperwork was concluded a cheque was handed to him. He then asked the representative what all the fuss was about and the man duly took off the bike's petrol cap and showed him the inscription, which read: 'To Jimmy Dean, love Elvis.' The Harley-Davidson had been a gift from the King to his favourite actor and had been Dean's most cherished possession. Experts had been looking for it for thirty years.

The World-famous Frozen Dead Grandpa

Back in 1994, a Norwegian by the name of Trygve Bauge was found to be living illegally in the small town of Nederland in Colorado, seventeen miles west of the city of Boulder. State officials soon deported Bauge back to his home-town of Oslo and locals began discussing the Norwegian and his unusual interest in cryonics, which is the freezing of dead people in the hope that scientific advances may make their revival and cure possible in future years. Needless to say, rumours began to spread and within a few weeks local police took a trip to Bauge's isolated and windswept property to have a look around.

Inside a rickety old shed behind the house officers found a five-foot high, thickly insulated wooden box and inside was the body of Bauge's grandfather, Bredo Morstoel, resting in a stainless-steel coffin and packed in dry ice. Further investigations revealed Morstoel had died of a heart attack in Norway five years earlier and his grandson had the body preserved, shipped to a cryonics centre in America and subsequently frozen. When his money began to run out and the storage fees increased, Bauge then collected his grandfather for storage in the shed behind his house. Unsurprisingly, the national media descended upon the small town on receiving news of the 'frozen dead guy'. A state judge swiftly passed a law preventing the further storage of dead bodies on private property and Bauge, from his new home in Oslo, threatened to 'sue until hell freezes over' if his grandfather was moved. In the meantime, he was paying local Nederlander Bo Shaffer $200 per month to drive an ice truck up to the shed to repack Grandpa and ensure he remained frozen. It turned out that under state law a dead person, frozen or otherwise, needs no visa to remain where he is and so the town had no way of evicting him.

Tales of the 'frozen dead guy' began circulating in earnest. Initially Tessa Warren, president of the Nederland chamber of commerce, was not amused, but soon she became aware of how the situation that had made her town famous across America could be used to their advantage. It all began as the millennium approached and, as locals thawed in their attitude towards the frozen man, a champagne millennium birthday party was arranged in his honour and Bo Shaffer, now known as the Ice Man, sold off parts of the original shed for $15 a time to tourists.

A year later, the first 'Frozen Dead Guy Day' was organized and tourists flocked into town to be greeted with frozen dead guy hats, T-shirts, postcards and posters, while Shaffer provided lamplight tours of the shed as champagne stands appeared in the yard close to Grandpa's resting place, all with the full blessing of his grandson Trygve Bauge at home in Norway, who believes it is a fun way to honour his grandpa while keeping Colorado a 'safe place for cryonics in the future'.

'It's like one of those things that never goes away, like a mole,' says Tessa Warren. 'People now associate Nederland with a frozen dead guy, and we can't make it disappear, so why not use it to create an economic opportunity for our town?'

Organizers expect this year's event (which includes a frozen T-shirt contest, a coffin race, a frozen brain contest, the 'Grandpa crawl' and even a Grandpa look-alike competition) could attract as many as 8,000 people to the area, more than five times the town's population. The festival has even appeared in the pages of the *Boston Globe*, *Sports Illustrated* and *National Geographic* and a gameshow network has broadcast the events for a *Games Across America* TV programme. And it all happened without spending a cent on advertising. I wonder what Grandpa will make of it all if he finally does wake up?

Suspended Animation

All of this reminds me of one of the most famous urban legends of all time – that Walt Disney had his body frozen and lies under what is now the

Pirates of the Caribbean exhibition in Disneyland, waiting for a cure for the lung cancer that killed him on 15 December 1966. This idea has been discussed worldwide for forty years with feature items and books supporting all manner of theories, one of which is that Disney was preoccupied with his own death and arranged to have himself frozen in a cryonic chamber filled with liquid nitrogen in order to wait until medical research had identified the cause of his illness. It is said the renowned creator of cartoons expected to be 'reanimated' himself one day.

But research has proved Disney was cremated two days after his demise and his death certificate, signed by embalmer Dean Fluss, confirms his remains are interred at the Forest Lawn Cemetery in Los Angeles. Urban legend fans insist the hasty burial and private ceremony point towards the famous animator's family covering up the real story of cryonic preservation, but if that was their clandestine intention, Disney insiders could easily have dispelled such notions by holding a public burial with an empty casket, throwing theorists off the scent completely. There are few, if any, investigators these days who still believe Disney's body is preserved in a frozen state, and his family have also gone on record to dispel such a theory by stating many years later that Uncle Walt simply did not want a public funeral. They also added that when he died he was unaware his illness was terminal, suggesting no alternative plans would have been made in any case.

What is known, however, is that according to the American Cryonics Society around one thousand members have made arrangements for cryopreservation, and it is thought over 100 people worldwide are currently in cryonic suspension. The great animator, it would appear, is not one of them.

Crate Expectations

What is known to be true, however, is the story of the man who shipped himself to his parents' address in a cargo crate. The *Washington Post* reported on 10 September 2003 the story of Charles McKinley, a 25-year-old New York warehouse worker, who decided to save on air travel costs by posting himself to his parents' home for a four-week holiday. Possibly inspired by Woodie Guthrie's folk song 'I'm Gonna Mail Myself to You', McKinley packed himself, some clothes, food and a laptop computer into a shipping crate with a label marked 'Saturday Special Delivery' pasted on the side. He then settled down and waited to be loaded on to a Boeing 727 at Newark International Airport, New York, with the $600 shipping costs being charged to his (presumably ex-) employer.

The Kitty Hawk Cargo Company aircraft

then made scheduled stops in Buffalo, New York and Fort Wayne, Indiana, where the crate was transferred on to another flight to his parents' hometown in Texas. The parcel was then received by Pilot Air Freight, a delivery company in Grapevine, Texas, before being driven to the McKinley household in DeSoto. The crazy scheme would probably have worked if McKinley hadn't become so excited by the idea of his plan working as well as it had that he kicked out the slats in the foot of the crate, jumped out and shook the delivery driver's hand in thanks. The driver, Billy Ray Thomas, responded by calling the police, who quickly attended the scene, verified the episode and then discovered McKinley had three outstanding warrants for his arrest, which is why he had taken off for New York in the first place. He was last heard of residing in DeSoto county jail and, although he was not charged in relation to his stunt, the story has alerted the authorities to the terrorist threat posed by cargo shipments, only 10 per cent of which are ever inspected.

McKinley himself, speaking to reporters, said he would 'never ever do such a thing again', adding that he had been 'cold and thirsty' during the fifteen-hour flight and that he didn't realize he might have a 'terrorist label' applied to him. Captain Phillip Beall of the Airline Pilots Security Alliance, a group supporting the call to arm all pilots, commented: 'Anyone can climb into a box that's properly packaged, as was demonstrated by this idiot.'

Idiot he may have been, but it was an ingenious idea and one that makes us wonder how many times a stunt like this has actually worked in the past, because if one has we are unlikely to know about it. But, a word of warning just in case you have been inspired to post yourself to the Bahamas or somewhere equally exotic. By chance, the crate was carried in a heated and pressurized storage hold. It could easily have been placed in one of the lower, un-pressurized compartments and that would have meant curtains for the enterprising Mr McKinley.

Train Reaction

A Hungarian newspaper reported the following story during the early 1970s. Cristo Falatti had been out motorcycling on a warm summer's evening when he approached a railway line just at the moment the crossing gates were lowered. As he sat waiting for the train to pass, a shepherd joined him, tied his goat to the crossing gate, folded his arms and also waited. Within a few minutes, a horse and cart had pulled up and was followed by a middle-aged man in an expensive sports car. A few minutes later, the train roared past, startling the horse, which then turned and bit Falatti on the shoulder. Angry and hot-tempered, Falatti reacted by punching the horse on the side of the head and the horse's owner then jumped from his cart and attacked Falatti. The horse, backing away from the commotion, crashed the cart into the front of the sports car, which meant the middle-aged driver also jumped out and joined the scuffle. This had all happened very quickly, and the shepherd, albeit shocked and confused, tried to calm the situation down and pacify all three men. At which point the crossing gate lifted up to allow the traffic to pass, hanging the shepherd's goat in the process. He, too, then joined the fight. The insurance companies are still trying to establish liability to this day.

Lady and the Tramp

A middle-aged and expensively dressed business-woman had fallen asleep on the London Underground. A tramp boarded the train, sat next to the gently snoring lady and also fell asleep, resting his head on her shoulder. Onlookers were disgusted to see him cough phlegm on to the lapel of her suit jacket, then wake up and leave the train. A few stops later, the lady also woke up and noticed the mess on her jacket. Embarrassed and assuming it was her own saliva, she quickly scooped it up with one finger and popped it into her mouth, glanced around the carriage in the hope nobody had noticed, then left at the next station.

Tight Jeans

Striving for the perfect fit, Levi Strauss introduced their popular shrink-to-fit range in the 1980s, leading to stories about a girl who had worn her new pair of Levi's in the bath to achieve the desired fit, but spent too long in the water and the jeans shrank so much she was found, crushed to death in the bath, by her parents. Variations on this legend include the fire brigade cutting the young girl out of her jeans to save her life and huge wads of cash apparently being paid in compensation by Levi to avoid legal action. The truth is there is no evidence of anybody being squeezed to death by their new jeans.

Blacks in America Lose the Right to Vote

One of the urban myths that has been circulating in America over recent years is that African Americans are soon to lose their hard-won right to vote in national or local elections. The reason given is that the Voting Rights Act of 1965, generally regarded as America's most successful piece of civil rights legislation, was introduced only for a trial period and is due to expire in 2007. However, the Voting Rights Act of 1965 was in fact introduced simply to enforce the 14th Amendment to the Constitution of the United States, passed as long ago as June 1866, Section One of which reads:

All persons born or naturalized in the United States, and subject to the jurisdiction thereof, are citizens of the United States and of the State wherein they reside. No State shall make or enforce any law, which shall abridge the privileges or immunities of citizens of the United States; nor shall any State deprive any person of life, liberty, or property, without due process of law; nor deny to any person within its jurisdiction the equal protection of the laws.

Amendment 15, passed on 3 February 1870, reinforced this by establishing the rights of all citizens to vote, stating in Section One:

The right of citizens of the United States to vote shall not be denied or abridged by the United States or by any State on account of race, colour, or previous condition of servitude.

But since then, and until the Civil Rights Movement led by Dr Martin Luther King and others swept America in the late 1950s and 1960s, many African Americans have found their rights denied in different ways, especially in the Southern States. For example, six of them – Alabama, Georgia, Louisiana, Mississippi, South Carolina, and Virginia – introduced the Literacy Requirement, resulting in many African Americans being unable to vote as they did not qualify. Finding election booths in white-only areas of racially segregated towns, with perimeters guarded by hostile white locals, also discouraged the few that did qualify. The Voting Rights Act of 1965 effectively outlawed such practice and also made provision for the Attorney General to appoint federal voting examiners to ensure that legally qualified persons were free to register for all elections, or to assign federal observers to oversee the conduct of elections in order to prevent voter intimidation or any other attempts at stopping minority groups from exercising their right to vote.

So the important point is to remember the Voting Rights Act didn't give African Americans the right to vote – they have had that since 1870. What it did was ensure their long-time constitutional right was available to them, as it was for all American citizens. The fact the Voting Rights Act is up for renewal in 2007 is academic as it is certain to be extended and most would regard it to be unnecessary these days anyway. Yet this urban legend has been circulating the web since 1997. The dissemination of ill-informed opinion on a grand scale is one of the dangers posed by the internet and the reason why a story like this can be believed by such huge numbers of people. The story is not a hoax and was never meant as one. People just got it wrong.

Quick-thinking Exam Cheats

A student was struggling to complete a difficult final exam paper and continued to write for a full six minutes after the adjudicator called time. After all the other students had handed in their papers, the adjudicator picked up their papers and turned to leave. At that point, the student rushed up to hand in his question paper only for the adjudicator to explain it would not be accepted and he would have to re-sit the exam in six months' time. The distraught student tried to reason with the man, but to no avail. As a last resort, the student loftily inquired, 'But, sir, don't you know who I am?' Relieved by the adjudicator's response: 'I have no idea at all, now would you please leave,' the student knocked all the papers out of the man's hand, buried his own among them and ran out, never to return. Well, there was no need to: rumour has it he received an A.

There are other examples of such audacity, which I obviously recommend you try, albeit at your own risk. On the East Coast of America a story is told of one student who, on arriving at his final exam, asked the adjudicator for two notebooks. Two hours later he handed one in, which had written on the first page: 'Dear Mum, I have just finished my final paper of the term and I am just writing to say I think it went really well.' The rest of the notebook was completely blank.

He then hurried home and, with the help of his textbooks, class notes and the internet, wrote the answers to the exam in the second notebook, then promptly posted it to his mother on the West Coast. His unsuspecting mother quickly posted the notebook back to his university professor with a letter explaining the obvious mix-up. The examiners took pity on him and marked the notebook, and he too received an A.

But scams like this do not always work, as four medical students found to their cost when they headed off for a weekend's fishing in Yorkshire prior to their exam on Monday. Having spent their last night in a casino, drinking and gambling, all four overslept and missed the exam. On the way back to college, the lads made up a story and explained to their professor that the reason for their absence was a punctured tyre, miles from the nearest town, which had meant a three-hour walk in the rain to call for help. The professor took pity on the lads and invited them back the following day to sit the paper in a specially convened examination. On arriving, all four were placed in separate rooms and given a two-part paper. The first, they were told, would make up 20 per cent of their mark and would take three hours. They were then given a second paper – to form the remaining 80 per cent of the overall mark, and to be completed in their own time. On it was written a single question: 'Which tyre was flat?'

ANIMAL CRACKERS

The Beast of Bodmin Moor

Tales have been told of a mysterious beast roaming Bodmin Moor ever since Sir Arthur Conan Doyle first published his Sherlock Holmes adventure *The Hound of the Baskervilles* in the *Strand Magazine* in 1901. The story centres on the fictional Baskerville Hall, located on Bodmin Moor in Cornwall, a bleak and sweeping expanse of open countryside that has inspired storytellers for generations. Conan Doyle used the moor, with its caves, sudden dips and treacherous bogs, as a backdrop for his tale of the ghostly hound that has reputedly terrorized the Baskerville family for several generations. Sherlock Holmes may have solved the mystery of the hound, but the legend of a beast on Bodmin has kept going. Over the years farmers have complained of livestock being slaughtered by a mysterious large animal, and since 1983 hundreds of reports have been made of a great cat-like creature roaming wild on the moor. In 1996, as media attention increased, over 300 sightings were recorded and the subject was hot news in the gossip magazines of the time. Locals remain convinced there are one or more large panther- or puma-like creatures loose on the moor, yet no solid evidence has ever been found. That in itself is not conclusive, of course, as a whole army could hide on Bodmin Moor without being detected, but you would think at least the odd carcass or dead body would have been found at some point over the many years this legend has been propagated. In 1994, a local farmer sold her entire flock of sheep after four ewes were mysteriously ripped to death one night. Despite the fact they were not eaten, as one might expect in the case of a hungry wildcat, the farmer has now become one of many dedicated to finding the Beast of Bodmin Moor.

Looking for ABCs (alien big cats) has become an obsession for such folk, somewhat reminiscent of the hunt for the Loch Ness Monster especially as, like Nessie, the ABCs remain undetected. During the mid 1990s, as reported sightings around Bodmin Moor increased, the government dispatched officials from the Ministry of Agriculture to investigate. Their report, published on 19 July 1995, concluded there was 'no verifiable evidence to be found to support the theory', while conceding that 'the investigation could not prove that a big cat is not present'. So that was a waste of time and money, then. Less than a week later, on 24 July, three brothers were walking by the river Fowey on the southern edge of the moor and found what turned out to be the skull of a large cat bobbing in the water. The skull was over seven inches long, complete with two large, prominent incisors and the discovery made the national news, particularly as it came just a week after the government report. However, the British Museum later confirmed that a tropical cockroach egg was found in the skull that could not possibly have been laid in Britain. They concluded the skull must have once been part of an old leopard-skin rug that had been imported to Britain.

In 1997, staff at Newquay Zoo identified tracks found to the south of the moor as those of a puma and shortly afterwards a now-famous photograph was produced of a large, black, cat-like creature, although the authenticity of this piece of evidence has not been confirmed. Then, in 1999, the government sent in the Royal Air Force, equipped with the latest military night vision equipment and thermal cameras, but bad weather hampered their operation (hardly surprising, since it was October) and nothing was found. Another complete waste of time and money.

The county of Surrey has also been the centre of ABC activity, with twenty-one sightings recorded in 2005 alone. Villagers in Abinger Common claim to have spotted on several occasions the puma that is supposed to have stalked villages south of Dorking. Surrey has been a favoured location for such sightings since 1959, when reports were first made of 'strange big cats' on the Surrey and Hampshire border. The local constabulary ignored the reports at the time, rather as their successors in the force dismiss reports of car theft and the like today, but those reporting the sightings were convinced. One of the most graphic accounts came from a Mr Burningham who, when driving along a secluded country lane one evening, saw what he described as an enormous cat crossing the road about forty yards in front of him. Mr Burningham stopped and watched as the beast, about the size of a Labrador dog but with a 'definite feline gait', crouched in woods watching lambs gambolling in a nearby field. After several minutes, the cat moved out of sight and Burningham drove away, only reporting his experience when the local press highlighted further sightings a few years later.

In 1962, there were two sightings of ABCs in the Shooters Hill district of London, the first by a lorry driver and the second by an on-duty police-man startled by what he thought to be a cheetah jumping over the bonnet of his patrol car. Other sightings in Surrey prompted a mass cheetah hunt across the county the following year, but no real evidence of ABC activity was found. Then, in 1964, Surrey residents reported terrible howling noises one night, unlike anything they had ever heard. A herd of cattle stampeded and the following morning a steer was found dead in nearby woods. The examining vet reported the wounds had been caused 'by an animal which was not to be found in this country'.

Surrey authorities denied the existence of wild cats roaming the countryside, although the general belief was that a private collector had released two or three puma cubs into the wild during the 1950s, either deliberately or by mistake, and these accounted for the sightings during that decade and the following one. There is no doubt the county provides the perfect conditions for such animals, being less harsh than Bodmin Moor, warmer, less windy and stocked with sufficient game and livestock to keep an adult cat alive for a long period of time. The presence of dense and remote stretches of woodland, coupled with the fact that pumas are nocturnal and afraid of humans, make it possible for such creatures to remain undetected for decades, if not for all time.

A survey by the British Big Cats organization supports the sightings in both Surrey and Bodmin Moor, stating: 'there is little doubt that big cats are roaming Britain.' There were 2,052 reported sightings in 2005 alone, the majority being in the southeast and southwest (i.e. Surrey and Bodmin Moor), but, despite evidence to suggest there have been many attacks on livestock in England by what appear to be big cats, no attacks on humans have been reported.

And so the hunt continues, but one thing is certain: like Nessie, Big Foot and the Abominable Snowman, without firm evidence to disprove their existence, the legends will persist and people will continue to believe in them. I feel it is time to put Sherlock Holmes on the case once again.

Black Widows' Pique

A Californian surfer had decided to book into a local hairdressing salon to have his Jamaican-style dreadlocks trimmed and tightened up. The unsuspecting hairdresser began to cut the ends and noticed a particularly lumpy dread towards the back of his head. As she attempted to thin it out, hundreds of tiny but deadly black widow spiders that had hatched from eggs laid on the man's head spilled out and attacked. Police later found hairdresser and surfer both lying dead in the salon after reports from passers-by.

Cockroach Cluster

I heard another insect egg-related legend, which I was assured was absolutely true, about a woman who worked in a post office in the north of England and was in the habit of licking the stamps instead of using the damp sponge provided. One day she made a small cut in her tongue on the edge of one of the stamps and, within a week, instead of healing there was a small lump growing. The following week it had grown to the size of a pea although the doctor assured her the swelling would go down after a course of antibiotics. A week later, at a routine check-up, her dentist suggested taking an X-ray of the lump. Unsure what he could see on the X-ray, the dentist made a small incision with his scalpel and a real-live cockroach crawled out. It had emerged from a cluster of eggs embedded in the glue of the stamp, which was then transferred on to the woman's tongue. 'Really – it's absolutely true!' I was assured. 'It even made the local television news.' Only, it didn't, did it. Of course the story isn't true – just one that's been repeated over the years in countries everywhere. Apparently it has even been on CNN news.

Cockroach eggs are laid in batches of around fourteen, although sometimes there can be up to fifty eggs, within a single egg case or 'ootheca'. Each cockroach grows into the size of an adult before eating its way out of the ootheca and into your furniture. Like most living things, they cannot survive in glue and won't be passed on to your tongue when you lick a stamp or envelope. Will I ever again believe anything I am told without first checking it for myself?

The Best-dressed Kangaroo in the Bush

A world-famous fashion photographer, who wishes to remain nameless, was in a convoy with four equally well-known international fashion models on their way to a photo-shoot location, deep in the Australian outback. Suddenly a full-sized kangaroo sprang from the bush and was knocked down by the lead vehicle. Everybody got out to see what had happened and found the motionless marsupial lying to the side of the four by four. The whole entourage was deeply upset, apart from the photographer who was not known to miss a photo opportunity when presented with one. Having calmed everybody down, the photographer removed his expensive Gucci leather jacket and dressed the kangaroo in it. He then propped the creature up against a eucalyptus tree and, with Ayers Rock in the background, began to take his pictures. The girls were uncomfortable with this opportunism but their mood lifted when it became obvious the animal was not dead and had merely been knocked unconscious. They found it hard to contain their laughter when the kangaroo regained full consciousness and bounced off at high speed into the bush, complete with Gucci leather jacket, containing the photographer's wallet, passport, tickets, keys and valuable rolls of film. None of the rest of the team, it is recorded, joined the photographer in his fruitless two-hour pursuit through the midday sun, preferring instead to watch the chase from their air-conditioned motor home, sipping ice-cold drinks from the fridge.

A Dog's Dinner

An elderly couple booked a table for a special treat at a completely authentic Taiwanese restaurant that had just opened in Birmingham, run by recent émigrés to Britain. The couple brought with them their beloved dachshund, which had been their faithful companion for over ten years and went everywhere with them. Taking their seat, they were handed menus by the head-waiter, who then pointed towards the dog. As he spoke no English, he gestured that he would happily take their pet to the kitchens, where the couple assumed he would be fed. The grateful couple laughed and agreed, commenting to each other about the kind gesture of the restaurant staff, who had by then scooped the little fellow up and taken him off. A short while later, after the wine had been poured and the conversation flowed, the dog was returned to them, only this time he had been fried in ginger and garlic and was being served up as a starter. Apparently it was common practice back in Taiwan for guests to bring their own starter to be prepared by the head chef.

The Choking Doberman

In another dog-related drama, a lady returned home from work to find her Doberman Pinscher lying on the kitchen floor choking and gasping for air. With the help of a neighbour, she loaded the pet into her car and rushed around to the veterinary surgeon, who examined the hound and decided to operate immediately. With that, the lady returned home with assurances from the vet that he would telephone later in the evening to let her know how things had gone. But she had barely walked through the door when the phone rang and the vet, clearly anxious, told her to get out of the house immediately and telephone the police. He then went on to explain that he had removed three human fingers from the dog's throat. Police later arrested a man with three missing digits hiding in her bedroom, obviously believing the dog was still waiting for him outside.

There's an Alligator in My Toilet

One of the most famous urban legends warns people of alligators in the sewers of New York

City. Apparently, wealthy residents often return home from sunshine holidays in Florida with baby alligators as pets. When they grow too large and are no longer wanted, residents simply flush them down the toilet and into the sewerage system where they can breed. Because of the lack of sunlight, the alligators are thought to have become blind and albino pale, creating a frightening image for anybody who believes alligators are alive and breeding under the manhole covers of Manhattan.

This story has become part of New York folklore and is unlikely to be true in modern times, but there is evidence to support the idea that alligators once did thrive in the sewers. In Robert Daley's book *The World Beneath Our Feet*, published in 1959, he quotes a former sewer superintendent called Teddy May who insisted he saw with his own eyes a number of alligators each about two feet long during a sewer inspection in 1935. His men had reported such creatures and May, deciding to have a look for himself, was amazed to find the reports to be true. May claims he immediately ordered the animals to be exterminated and his men, armed with rifles and pistols, set about the task. Within a month they were all gone.

The Lemming Myth

For many years we have been led to believe, or at least I have, that lemmings have a natural instinct to follow each other towards disaster and self-destruction. (Not unlike politicians really – it's never just one, is it?) According to this belief, lemmings, from time to time, will throw themselves en masse from the cliff-tops and into the sea in a bizarre demonstration of solidarity that has so far remained unexplained – until now, that is. The truth is that lemmings do no such thing. There are times when huge population increases will result in mass migration and provide us with images of millions of the little animals on the move, but they do not head naturally towards disaster. Along the way, some will inevitably be pushed by the seething hordes to their destruction, but such deaths will be accidental rather than self-propelled. In fact, when faced with competition for mating partners and food, lemmings are far more likely to kill each other than to leap into oblivion.

To find the source of the myth we need to turn to the 1958 Walt Disney movie *White Wilderness*, which was filmed in Alberta, Canada, far away from the natural habitat of the lemming. The animals were in fact bought by the film makers from Inuit children in Manitoba and imported to the area for the scenes in which they starred. During filming, the rodents were placed on a large snow-covered turntable and photographed from every angle to simulate a migration sequence, and although the scenes of mass migration are impressive, only a few dozen lemmings were ever present. The creatures were then herded over the rocks and into the river below (tight camera work made it look like the sea), as if to their deaths. Nine different photographers spent three years assembling the images. By the way, lemmings can swim, so the scenes of dead rodents floating out to sea would seem to point to skulduggery during the making of the film. They are undoubtedly the cause of the widespread, completely erroneous, belief that lemmings commit suicide in vast numbers when their population becomes too large.

Hammerhead Hamster

Workmen had just finished laying a carpet in the basement of a customer's house and decided to step on to the patio for a cigarette. One of them was annoyed to find his packet missing from the top pocket of his shirt and the other pointed out a bulge in the newly laid carpet. Annoyed at having left his packet on the floor and then carpeted over it, he was reluctant to lift the carpet back up again. Instead he took a hammer and flattened the lump smooth. That night, as he and the other carpet layers packed up their tools, the workman noticed his cigarette packet on the dashboard of their van. The following morning when they arrived for work, their customer asked them, 'Have you seen our pet hamster? He was in the room you were working in, but Johnny left his cage door open, and now we can't find him anywhere.'

The Magic Rabbit

A young couple had moved into a cottage in the Gloucestershire countryside next door to a family with children who kept an elderly white angora rabbit to which they were devoted. The family was due to go away for a long weekend at Euro Disney and asked their new neighbours

to keep an eye on things for them. All seemed quiet until the final morning when the couple's dog came sauntering up the garden with the muddy corpse of the rabbit hanging from its mouth. As there were no teeth marks or blood, they assumed their dog had broken the rabbit's neck and decided to shampoo its fur, dry it off and place it carefully back in the hutch in the garden, hoping the family would assume the bunny had died of natural causes over the weekend.

When the family returned the following day, the young couple kept a deliberately low profile until the father dropped in for a chat. Visibly nervous, the couple asked how the trip had gone. 'Very well, thanks,' came the reply, 'but the strangest thing has happened. The kids' pet rabbit died on the day we left, so we buried it in the back garden, by the fence. Then this afternoon we returned to find it back in its hutch, as clean as a whistle.'

Although this urban myth may well have some truth to it, it is a story that has appeared in many forms, including one in which the neighbours replace the dead rabbit with an identical live one, and others involving dogs, cats or other pets.

The Elephants' Graveyard

One of the most enduring legends suggests that when an old elephant senses death is imminent, it will separate from its herd and trek alone to the ancestral graveyard where it will settle and wait to pass over to that great circus in the sky. Instinct, people were told, led elephants to a final, hidden resting place, and during the nineteenth century all expeditions to Africa sought evidence of elephant graveyards. None were ever found. Palaeontologists still hope to find ancient grave-yards, deep in the bush and excellently preserved, but they are yet to be discovered, and while they remain undiscovered the myth will no doubt continue to be perpetuated. Large collections of elephant remains have been discovered in the past, but Dr Karen McComb of the University of Sussex claims this is more likely to be the result of disease or fire decimating a herd.

On the other hand, elephants are known to be

aware of their dead and to show an interest in deceased herd members in a way no other creature on earth does, apart from humans and chimpanzees. Chimps display close affection for a dead family member and will stay with the body, only losing interest as decomposition begins to set in. But elephants will continue to visit the grave of a herd member and appear to remember their dead by displaying signs of grieving. In 2003, the Savute Lion Pride in Botswana killed a mature bull elephant at a waterhole close to the Savute camp, a rare event, and the dramatic scenes that followed were closely recorded.

As the pride of lions gathered to feed on the carcass, a bull elephant from the same herd moved towards them, flared his ears and chased the pride away with a series of short charges. The lions moved to a safe distance and the elephant began touching and stroking the stricken beast from top to toe for some time, appearing, as some observers noted, to be paying his respects to his fallen friend. It is obvious then that elephants are like people in some respects, hence the notion that elephants 'never forget'. Naturally they do, just as we do, but their 'elephantine' power of recall is undoubtedly vital to their survival.

There have also been reports of elephants gathering up the scattered bones of their dead and piling them up on one spot, thereby feeding the burial-ground myth. Extensive research has shown that when presented with the skulls of an elephant, buffalo and rhino, members of a herd of elephants will pay great attention to the elephant skull, while ignoring the other two. Clearly they show an interest in their dead and will go out of their way to visit elephant remains, but there is no evidence of any ancient grave-yards. As for elephants being scared of mice, that's just another myth.

Dog Daze

In a small village, close to Killarney in Southern Ireland, the new local priest was doing the rounds of his parish and introducing himself to the local families along the way. Unsurprisingly, he was keen to make a good impression and had, so far, received a warm welcome. Along the lane from the church he came across a family home with a large playful dog romping in the front garden. Being an animal lover, he spent a short time playing with the hound before walking to the front door. When the lady of the house invited him in, the dog slipped inside and the children of the family were soon also playing with the animal. The priest noticed the dog was making quite a mess and had left its muddy paw prints all around the lounge where he was sitting having a conversation with the adults of the household. Tea was served, but as the dog smelt as if it had been rolling in something unpleasant the priest, distracted by the stench, rather lost his appetite. The hungry hound then stuck his nose into the plate of biscuits on the coffee table and lapped them all up in seconds before cocking his leg to relieve himself against a table leg. The priest, noticing the family's growing discomfort, decided to leave before the dog became even more embarrassing and, making his way to the door, he commented, 'It's a lively dog you have yourselves there.' To which the father of the family replied, 'Our dog? It's not our dog. We thought he was yours.'

ON BOTH SIDES OF THE LAW

Mystery Tickets

A man and his wife had just returned home from dinner with friends to find their expensive Mercedes had been stolen. Naturally upset, they telephoned the police to report the theft and even went out in their second car to see if they could find the Mercedes. After a fruitless search, they returned home and went to bed. The following morning, the Merc had been returned with an anonymous note on the windscreen apologizing for taking the car, stating it had been an emergency and enclosing two expensive theatre tickets in the envelope. The couple were confused but pleased to have their car back in good condition so shrugged the incident off as strange but harmless. However, when they returned from the theatre a few weeks later, they found their house empty of all possessions and a note reading: 'We hope you enjoyed the play.'

Neighbourhood Watch

A story is told in Florida, USA, of a man who was so concerned about car thieves in his area that he used to chain his sports car to two trees in his front yard every night as an extra security measure. The car was also fitted with an alarm, tracker system and immobilizer. One morning, however, he woke up to find his car still chained to the trees, only facing in the opposite direction. On closer inspection, he discovered a note placed under a windscreen wiper. The note read: 'When we want it, we will take it.'

Tarts for Afters

Stories of police entrapment are always popular and even more fun when they turn out to be true. In the early 2000s, the Reuters news agency reported a story from Shanghai about just such an entrapment operation, in which police in the Chinese eastern province of Jiangsu were said to be abusing their authority. Armed with a 6,000 yuan (approximately £400) expense fund, deputy chief Gao Mingliang opened a brothel disguised as a restaurant and instructed waitresses to entice customers into the back rooms for the off-menu 'desserts'. However, after a short time, Mingliang's men would raid the premises and arrest businessmen in the secret back rooms who had opted for the Steaming Pears with Egg Custard Tarts to round off their meals. Once down at the local station, customers would be fined and, if the haul was a good one, the girls would be paid a performance bonus.

Apparently the deputy chief made nearly £5,000 in profit from the business before neighbouring police became suspicious and arrested the man named as the restaurant owner, sentencing him to a year in a labour camp for running a brothel. Aggrieved at his treatment, the owner made a full statement to government officials, who set their own trap, caught Mingliang with his trousers down (metaphorically speaking) and sent him to jail for a year.

Police Shocker

Two police officers were patrolling a car park at night when they spotted a car with no lights on, apart from the interior light. The young trainee went to investigate and found a teenage couple having sex in the back seat. Unsure how to handle the situation, he returned to the veteran officer to ask for advice and was told, 'Do what I always do, just tell them you will arrest them for indecency unless we can both have a turn too, one after the other . . . You can go first.'

After ten minutes or so, the young policeman returned to the car with a self-satisfied smirk and the older man strolled across to take his turn. As he reached the car, however, he shone his torch at the trembling girl. It was his own sixteen-year-old daughter.

No Smoke without Fire

An American lawyer was given a box of twenty-four rare and expensive Cuban cigars by a grateful client and made sure they were included in his insurance policy, which covered flood, fire and theft. Within a few months, he had smoked all of the cigars and then made a cheeky claim on his insurance, maintaining they had been 'lost in a series of small fires'. The insurance company refused to pay, for obvious reasons, but the lawyer, having read through the terms and conditions of his policy, took them to court. It seems he was the only person not to be surprised when he won his case: despite the judge agreeing with the insurance company that the claim was tenuous, he still ruled the policy did indeed cover small fires. Faced with an expensive appeal process, which they were in no way certain of winning, the insurance company accepted the ruling and agreed to a compensation payment of $15,000 to the lawyer. However, immediately after the payment had been accepted, the insurance company had the lawyer arrested on twenty-four counts of arson and he was later convicted on his own evidence of intentionally burning his own property and sentenced to twenty-four months in prison with a $24,000 fine.

Hypnotic Bank Robber

Stories have been circulating about a bank robber who used hypnosis to trick bank staff into handing over the equivalent of tens of thousands of pounds in cash. It was a major Russian newspaper that published the news item, suggesting local police in Moldova had claimed the thief was a trained hypnotist from Russia. Apparently he would begin talking to the cashier, gradually inducing a trance and then bring him or her back to consciousness before leaving so that nobody, including other customers, would be any the wiser. Huge discrepancies would be found in the tills at the end of the day as a result of what would appear to be the perfect crime. Many European banks became so concerned about the problem, they instructed staff not to look customers in the eye for fear of copy-cat thefts. Others were a little more sceptical about the whole thing.

According to a leading British hypnotherapy website, individuals have to be in a receptive

state of mind in order to be hypnotized. It also makes the point that if it were possible to hypnotize people without their knowledge, they would still be able to refuse suggestions and reject requests being made of them.

This is still a good story, however, suggesting other situations where hypnotizing strangers without their knowledge could come in handy. For a start, the police could hypnotize every criminal suspect and have them admit to their misdemeanours. But that might work both ways as guilty suspects could also hypnotize the police to get themselves released without charge. If it were possible to hypnotize people without their consent and get them to act in ways they would later have no recollection of, then one thing is certain: there would be a lot more people learning how to do it – starting with me.

Who's the Mugger Now?

Walking along a crowded street in Sheffield, a respectable businessman collided with a passer-by, only to discover shortly afterwards that his wallet was missing. Believing his pocket had been picked, he looked for the man in the crowds and, spotting him, gave chase. He caught up with the passer-by in a side street and proceeded to beat him up. Unable to find the wallet, despite frisking the passer-by all over, he concluded the man must have dumped it after stealing the money, so he took all the man's cash and went on his way. On arriving home, he saw in front of him, on the hall table, his own wallet, which he had forgotten to take out with him when he left in the morning. The victim had become the mugger.

Electricity Meter Fraud

Electricity meter readers in London were baffled when they started finding pools of water in the electricity meters on a university campus. They called in plumbers and carried out exhaustive tests in an attempt to put a stop to what could prove to be extremely hazardous. Students were interviewed and surveillance was introduced but the problem persisted and no answer could be found. Until one day a student was caught red-handed. As the lad paid his meter, the inspector rounded the corner to see him close the cupboard and go back to his room. A few minutes later, the meter was checked and found to be empty apart from the usual puddle of water so the lad was arrested and questioned by police. It was then revealed that a student doing a degree in fine arts had carved out perfect moulds for fifty pence pieces. These were filled with water, placed in the freezer overnight and then used by a group of students to top up the electricity meters before the fake coins melted.

Ice Bullets

In another tale of ingenuity with ice, police in London were investigating the death of an underworld figure in what they had presumed had been a gangland killing. The body of the victim had received five shots to the head and body but there were no exit wounds and nothing at the scene of the crime that could be used as forensic evidence. With no evidence and nothing for the ballistic experts to work with, the crime remained unsolved. However, an informer later gave police information that a gang had found a way to create bullet-shaped ice cubes that could be used to kill a victim and the evidence would then simply melt away. This story has been told for decades and conspiracy theorists have also suggested that the mystery second gunman in the assassination of President John Kennedy in 1963 used ice bullets, which would explain those wounds to the President not allegedly caused by Lee Harvey Oswald (see 'The President's Brain is Missing').

However, ballistic experts have carried out extensive research on this subject and nobody has ever been able to fire an iced bullet in laboratory conditions. The heat from the gun melts the ice, even when chemically frozen to an ultra-low temperature, and a spurt of water dribbles from the barrel.

Maximum High

Drug dealers keep finding increasingly inventive ways of smuggling their contraband into Britain, but the tale of one young man should serve as a warning. In an attempt to bring a roll of LSD tablets into the country, a university student decided the best way to do so would be to seal it inside a condom and swallow the package. Once in Britain he would then let nature take its course, retrieve the drugs and sell them on for a huge profit. Unfortunately for him, the condom burst during the flight and the entire roll of LSD melted into his stomach. He is now being held at a secure psychiatric centre and firmly believes he is a giant red teapot.

Drugs Surprise

A community police officer was giving a lecture to young schoolchildren on Moss Side in Manchester. Producing a genuine cannabis joint and placing it in a dish, he passed it around the children so that they could see what it looked like and get used to how it smelt. The idea was that introducing children to drugs at such a young age would enable them to recognize drugs and avoid using them in the future. Naturally he warned them that if the dish was empty when it was given back, he would have to search them all before they left class. However, when the dish was passed back to him he was surprised to find that not only was the joint still in its place but it had been joined by three other types of drug – a packet of angel dust, one wrap of cocaine and a rock of crack. Clearly none of the children wanted to risk being searched.

TV Raid

Filming was taking place for a popular television crime series in a small English village. With the increased activity in the area, local residents had become used to talking to the film crew and had been discussing possible locations with them or, in the case of shopkeepers, were being compensated for loss of trade, while some were paid for the use of their property. One morning, the local jeweller was approached by a man with a clipboard and headset and asked if a robbery scene could be filmed in his premises. Naturally flattered and hoping the scene would be good for business, the man accepted a cheque for £2,000 and the film crew moved into position. The filming went beautifully as young men in cartoon-character masks burst into the shop, filled their bags with jewels and rushed back out into a waiting car. They then disappeared along the high street in a plume of rubber smoke. In the ensuing excitement, nobody in the village noticed the bogus film crew melt away and the man with the clipboard disappear. The real film crew claimed to have had no idea who the men were. Nobody ever returned with the jewellery and the cheque turned out to be a forgery.

Four by Four Runs over Four

Car jacking, during which armed men force drivers out of their expensive cars at gunpoint before stealing them, has become a major problem in some parts of the world. South Africa is one such country and many drivers in rural areas have begun to arm themselves, or at least to be extremely cautious. In one case, a mother was taking her children home in her off-roader when she came across an injured man lying in the road by his motorcycle. The rider had apparently been knocked off and was waving for attention, seeming to be in great pain. The woman slowed but decided not to stop completely. Instead, by instinct, she swerved on to the verge, sped through the bumpy long grass and hurried along to the nearest town to report the accident at the nearest police station. Officers rushed to the scene but could find no trace of the motorcyclist anywhere. Closer inspection revealed the car's tracks in the grass and police decided to investigate further. There, hidden in the long grass, were the bodies of four armed men who had been crushed to death. Police concluded they had been lying in wait for the young mother and she had killed all four without realizing it when she drove along the verge.

Drunken Decoy

Locals in a remote village in Cornwall were planning to celebrate the millennium together by holding a big party at the only pub in the village. As most of them would have to drive to the pub from their remote homes and ordering enough taxis would be impossible, there was a strong chance of many being caught driving with excess alcohol in their systems, especially as the new local bobby was an unfriendly and overly vigilant sort of chap. As expected, the policeman was on duty, waiting in the pub car park and watching as the first reveller staggered out at around 2 a.m., tripped and fell flat on his face. The policeman then observed him struggle to his feet and weave across the car park, fumbling for his keys, before resting both hands on the car bonnet to try and steady himself. He then got into the driver's seat, jerked the car into gear and kangarooed across the car park towards the exit. Having seen enough, the policeman drove forwards to block the exit, his blue lights flashing. Opening the car door, the driver crashed to the ground, and was promptly arrested and taken off to the local police station. However, on arrival he asked, quite lucidly, 'What have you arrested me for, officers?' On being told he was under caution for driving with excess alcohol, he then stated that he didn't touch alcohol and

hadn't had a drink in fifteen years. The police officers refused to believe him and, having carried out the usual tests, were amazed to find there was not a single drop of alcohol in his system. The police had no choice other than to release him but later suspected he had been the designated decoy for the evening. All the other partygoers shot off home as soon as the policeman had left with his fake 'drink driver'.

Good Neighbours

An American family had recently moved to an expensive part of the suburbs and found their new neighbours to be kind and friendly. But on returning home from a weekend away, they were distraught to find they had been burgled and many expensive items had been taken, including jewellery. When they asked their neighbours if they had seen or heard any suspicious activity, one of them, a softly spoken and well-dressed man in his early forties, advised them not to report the matter to the police. Instead he offered to make a few phone calls to see if there was anything he could do. The following morning all the missing items were neatly piled up in the front porch with an anonymous note of apology. They later accidentally discovered their neighbour to be a leading Mafia don and one of the most feared men in America. Nobody messed with him. The story, whether true or not, has been told since the 1930s.

Speed-trap Warning

A policeman had set up a mobile speed camera on a stretch of road between Woking and Guildford, hoping to spend the afternoon issuing speeding fines. The road had a long downhill sweeping bend, giving drivers little or no time to slow down before the camera, frequently set up on this stretch of road, had snapped its evidence. But on this occasion the policeman failed to catch a single driver as motorists cruised along well within the speed limit. After three hours without success, he packed up his equipment and headed back to the police station. As he drove along, he noticed a teenager sitting beside the road with a bucketful of money and a large notice reading: 'Thank you for your generosity.' As there was no law against this, there was little the officer could do about it except ponder how the lad had managed to obtain so much money from passing motorists. That was until he rounded the next corner and noticed a second youth with a big sign reading: 'Warning – Police Speed Trap Ahead: Payment for Tip-off Gratefully Received.' Apparently the two lads drove around most days looking for speed traps and, when they found one, took up their positions. They were making a small fortune.

Wheel Theft

In downtown New York, two youths noticed a parked car being jacked up at the front. Believing the car was about to have its wheels stolen, they started jacking up the rear to do the same thing when a man appeared and asked them what they were doing. 'It's OK, buddy,' said one of the youths, thinking this was a fellow thief. 'We will help you with the wheels as long as we can have the car stereo.' 'But it is my car, I am just fixing a puncture at the front,' replied the man. The boys then ran off, shouting: 'In that case, you can keep the stereo.'

Bang to Rights

A young couple had set up home in Nottingham but found after only three weeks of living in the area they had been burgled no less than four times. The husband worked for a security and surveillance company so his boss agreed to let him set up CCTV cameras for a few weeks in the hope of catching the villains. As expected, their home was broken into for a fifth time and the cameras captured perfect images of the criminals. Pleased with his work, the security expert handed the images in to the local police station and was not surprised to see uniformed officers on his doorstep later in the day. He assumed they had come to give him news of an arrest but, instead, they arrested him, then confiscated nine large marijuana plants growing in his front room. The plants could clearly be seen in the background of the images he had given the police.

FAMILY MATTERS

Through the Porthole

During the first months of the Second World War, a young mother decided to leave London and return home to Ireland where she would feel much safer. She took with her a six-year-old

daughter and two-year-old son, but on the ferry the youngster refused to settle in his bunk for the night. In desperation she threatened to 'put him out of the porthole' if he didn't stop crying and that seemed to work as the toddler quietened down. With that she went into the dining room for an evening meal but when she returned the porthole was open, the boy was missing and the little girl sleeping peacefully in her bunk after apparently carrying out her mother's threat.

Surprise Party

A local bank manager arrived at work in a filthy mood. It was his fortieth birthday but nobody at home had remembered. His wife had not mentioned it and their children set out for school without saying a word about their father's big day. There had been no cards in the post and not a single present, and that set the tone for the day. But his secretary had left him a nice card and small present on his desk, which cheered him up no end. With that he decided to invite her out to lunch and booked the most expensive restaurant in town. They had a wonderful meal and a little too much wine as they continued through the afternoon. Finally, on leaving the restaurant at 5 p.m., the secretary announced she was tipsy and wanted to go straight home. After he had driven her to her house, she invited her boss inside and told him to wait in the lounge as she had a surprise for him in the bedroom. As she disappeared from view he was left in no doubt about her intentions, so he quickly undressed and, clad in nothing but his boxer shorts, awaited her return. Unfortunately for him it was his wife who came in, along with their children, friends and members of the bank staff. His secretary and wife had arranged a surprise party to celebrate his birthday.

Old Spice

A middle-aged couple from Norfolk had retired and emigrated to India, taking their elderly father with them but leaving their grown-up children back in England. As the years passed, many a family holiday was spent in the warm climate and Christmas on the beach became a regular feature. One day the couple's eldest son and his wife received a sealed tin by recorded delivery inside which was a grey powder that they both agreed smelt and tasted exotic. They used the spice in their cooking until the following week when they received a letter from the son's parents asking for confirmation that they had received Grandfather's ashes and had scattered them in his favourite park as he had requested.

No Smoking in the Toilets

During a family barbecue one summer's after-noon, the father, who had been drinking all day, slipped and badly twisted his ankle. A family friend duly took him to hospital to have his ankle X-rayed while, back home, the injured man's wife began to clear up the patio. Noticing the bottle of fire-lighting fluid was nearly empty, she poured the remaining contents into the outside toilet before throwing away the empty container. When her husband returned home, he sat out on the patio nursing his bandaged ankle while his wife continued cleaning up the kitchen. A short while later, feeling the call of nature, he staggered over to the outside toilet, sat down and lit himself a cigarette. By the time he noticed the smell of fire-lighting fluid, it was too late and the resulting explosion blew the door off, while the man spent the next three months in hospital with serious burns.

The Secret Message

During the Second World War, a young soldier from Nottinghamshire had been posted to the Far East to fight the Japanese. Every week, with-out fail, he would send a letter to his mother to reassure her and let her know how he was. Then one week her regular letter failed to arrive and she began to worry. There was no letter the following week either, but by the weekend she had received a note from the War Office informing her he had been captured by a Japanese patrol and was being held as a prisoner of war. Officials assured her he was safe and would not be mistreated in any way and she was relieved. For her son the war was over. She was proud he had served his country and survived. A few weeks later, however, she received another letter from her son, which read: 'Dear Mother. Try not to worry about me as they are treating us well. I will be home as soon as the war is over. Please make sure little Gerald gets this stamp for his collection. Love you, John.'

The lady was delighted to hear the news but confused, as she had no idea who little Gerald was. Intrigued, she decided to steam the stamp off the envelope and found written on the back of the stamp the words: 'Mum, they have cut off my legs.'

Dumped on from a Great Height

On arriving home from work, a Scottish couple found a large hole in the roof of their bungalow, the furniture covered in a foul-smelling liquid and their pet dog lying dead in the middle of the front room. Puzzled and upset, they called in the

police who began an investigation. After a few
days the police returned to the bungalow with an
explanation. They had discovered that a passing
jumbo jet had ruptured a lavatory chemical
waste tank and the contents had spilled out at
30,000 feet. It froze in the atmosphere and then
fell to earth at great speed, smashing through the
roof of the couple's home, killing the dog and
then defrosting all over their possessions.

Naughty Photos

An elderly gentleman had taken a roll of film into
a processing shop so that it could be developed.
The following morning, as he returned to collect
his pictures, he was surprised to find himself
arrested by four police officers and bundled out
of the shop and into a waiting van. He was then
taken down to the local police station and
charged with possessing pornographic photographs of young children. The terrified old man
was held in the station cells until his lawyer
turned up and the problem was resolved. The
children in the photographs had been his own
grandchildren who had borrowed his camera
without him knowing to take pictures of each
other's bare bottoms for a joke.

Caught on Camera

A young French couple were married at a large, expensive ceremony with a lavish reception. Both families had a wonderful day and danced late into the evening. At one point the bride's father had taken off his jacket and left it hanging on his chair at the top table before returning to the dance floor. As the evening drew to a close, he picked up his jacket and reached in for the £5,000 in cash he had withdrawn to pay for the evening bar bill, but found it missing.

Clearly somebody at the reception must have stolen the money. The bride's father was horrified but, not wishing to destroy his daughter's big day, he decided not to tell her, while the groom's father offered to pay half of the bill with his credit card. The two sets of parents decided not to sour the whole event by bringing in the police, agreeing to keep the matter between themselves.

Once the young couple were away on their honeymoon, the bride's parents invited the groom's parents round to their house for dinner to review the first cut of the wedding video. The jokes about each other's dancing skills suddenly dried up when they noticed the cameraman had zoomed in on the bridegroom sitting alone at the top table. The stunned foursome stared at

the TV screen in silence as he reached inside his
father-in-law's jacket, removing the cash and
stuffing it into his own suit pocket.

THIS SPORTING LIFE

Football Fanatic

The following story is a tale I have heard at many football stadiums over the years. The fact that the same story, with a few slight modifications such as the names of the football clubs, is told again and again as if it were true elevates it from mere rumour or joke to the status of urban legend. It goes something like this. Chelsea were playing Manchester United in one of the most keenly awaited cup matches in recent memory. During the first half, a couple of fans noticed that the elderly gentleman sitting in front of them had an empty seat next to him and, as the game had been a complete sell-out, asked the old chap at half-time who had not turned up for the game. 'That is my wife's seat,' he told them. 'We have been coming to see United for fifty-three years; not missed a single match in all of that time. But unfortunately she died last week so I am on my own today for the first time in my life.' The fans felt for the old man and asked him if there were no other members of the family who could have accompanied him on such an emotional day. 'Ay, sure there are, laddie,' said the old fellow. 'But they are all at the funeral.'

Half-time Relief

The following exchange has gone down in football folklore, often as a joke, but still told in earnest about many different footballers and their managers. The original exchange can be traced to January 1973 in the dressing room at Wembley as England prepared to take on Wales. The national team manager Sir Alf Ramsey said to Rodney Marsh, a Manchester City player making his ninth international appearance: 'Rodney, this is your last chance to play for England. I will be watching you for the first forty-five minutes and if you don't work hard enough I will

pull you off at half-time.' To which Marsh replied, 'Christ, Alf, at Man City all they give us is an orange and a cup of tea.'

Ramsey, a strict disciplinarian, didn't appreciate this and that was the last game Marsh, a gifted striker, ever played for England. Ramsey confirms the exchange in his autobiography and Rodney Marsh has since admitted publicly that making the joke may have cost him his England career.

Sky Diving

In the mid 1990s a story circulated in America of the mystery surrounding the aftermath of a forest fire in California. Such fires are common during the hot, dry summer months and are usually not the subject of conversation across the land, but one such fire held a puzzle that needed solving. Inspecting the aftermath of a small but raging blaze, fire marshals discovered the badly charred body of a man in his twenties dressed in full scuba-diving gear, including the melted remains of a wetsuit, facemask and flippers, and burned and flattened air tanks. Given that the discovery was made a full fifteen miles from the nearest coast, it was apparent the chap was not on his way to a diving centre when he died. Foul play being suspected, a post-mortem was held which revealed the man had not died from either

drowning or burns, but from massive internal injuries. A full investigation began and, after dental records revealed his identity and his next of kin were informed, the mystery of the scuba diver in a smouldering forest began to be unravelled.

On the day of the fire, the deceased had been out diving in the Pacific Ocean and had already completed two successful dives when he entered the water for a third time. Meanwhile, fifteen miles away, fire fighters battling to control a routine blaze which was in danger of spreading to nearby homes, called in a fleet of helicopters to douse the area with water. The fire helicopters all carried large buckets beneath them, which were dipped into the ocean for rapid filling before being flown to the fire and emptied. The inevitable couldn't have happened, could it? Well, according to legend, it did. One minute the diver was peacefully enjoying the underwater scenery and the next he found himself in a fire bucket half a mile in the air. Presumably he then endured a terrifying airborne journey before being released with the sea water among the burning trees.

Apparently divers and pilots alike are warned of this story and encouraged to be alert at all times. Divers are advised to remain calm if they are hooked out of the water and to hang on to the bucket when the water is released. None the less, it strikes me there is still something fishy about this urban legend and I cannot foresee a day when parachutes become standard equipment for scuba divers.

Flaw in the Horse Box

A well-known trainer of racehorses had decided to race one of his favourite, but ageing, mares for the final time. On the morning of the race, he attempted to lead the horse into the trailer but the stubborn creature refused to budge. In the end, she had to be dragged in and the ramp was closed behind her. On the way to the race course, the horse crashed about in the box and made a frightful noise but the trainer ignored the distraction and continued his journey. When they arrived, the trainer was mortified to find the mare's legs had broken through the rotten floor of the horsebox and, although she had galloped along as best she could to keep up, had been horribly lacerated by the fast-moving surface of the road.

The Exploding Hound

During the 1950s, a group of duck hunters found their favourite lake completely frozen over during a cold snap in late January. Undaunted, one of the men decided to use dynamite to blow open a hole in the ice in the hope of attracting their prey to the area. However, misfortune was once again in evidence as the hunters' labrador retriever raced across the ice, collected the dynamite stick complete with lighted fuse and returned to the group of men who were, by then, scattering in all directions and screaming at the hound to 'sit', to no avail of course, although a mighty hole was made in the ice by the resulting explosion. But, as in all good urban legends, variations have evolved over the years.

In a modern version of the tale, two unlucky duck hunters have pulled on to the thick ice in their brand new $40,000 Lincoln Navigator, intending to use it as a warm observation point while waiting for the ducks to arrive. On throwing the dynamite and seeing the dog retrieve it, one of the hunters tries to shoot the dog, but the size-eight buckshot merely wounds the animal and, in its confused state, it then takes cover under the Lincoln. The pair, fortunately not in the car at the time, can only watch while their transport, supplies, means of communication, and shelter, not to mention their lunch, disappear to the bottom of the lake in a matter of seconds as the dynamite blows a hole beneath the vehicle. The eventual fate of the two men remains unknown.

Golfers, Beware!

There is a story sweeping the fairways of England that tells of a golfer who was in the habit of licking his golf ball clean after completing each hole. It is common for golfers to do this, but in this unfortunate chap's case he managed to pick up some weed killer that had been sprayed close to one of the lakes. This apparently contained a strong poison, which led to grave illness and the subsequent amputation of the golfer's legs. It is not known if this urban legend is true, but it is

most likely based on a true story, from Ireland, of a 65-year-old golfer who was admitted to hospital suffering from severe stomach cramps and was diagnosed with hepatitis, apparently triggered by ingesting weed killer at his local golf club where, as he informed his baffled doctors, he often licked his golf balls clean while out on the course. There have also been cases of liver disease traced to the poisons used in herbicides, pesticides and fertilizers sprayed by most golf clubs. So golfers, be warned. Do not lick your balls. Have your caddy lick them for you.

Bad Loser

While not usually dangerous, golf can be a frustrating game, and the true character of your opponent can be revealed during an afternoon on the golf course. One man worth avoiding in any situation would be the golfer who lost a friendly match by missing a putt on the last green. The game over, he shook his opponent's hand, picked up his own golf bag and threw it into the lake before storming off. Other golfers watched from the clubhouse as he sheepishly returned, waded into the water and retrieved his bag. He then fumbled through the pockets and fished out his car keys and wallet before throwing the clubs back in for the second time and driving off. Now, there is a man who doesn't think things through properly.

False Trail

For centuries fox hunting has been a major pastime throughout Britain, its popularity matched by equally strong opposition to it. During the nineteenth century there was one English lord who was firmly opposed to the hunting of foxes and resented groups of people riding all over his land with their hunting dogs. So, in an early attempt at hunt sabotage, he paid one of his farm workers a few extra shillings to lay a trail of aniseed leading right away from his land in the hope the hounds would follow the false trail instead of the fox. On the morning of the hunt, the lad did exactly what was asked of him and laid a strong trail leading away from his master's fields, through wooded glades, over hedges, through meadows and past a fast-flowing river. After several hours he decided to take a break and settled down in a country pub, miles from the estate, for lunch and a few pints of ale. Before long the distant sound of barking dogs could be heard and the lad grinned to himself as they came closer and closer. His plan had clearly worked, but he soon became alarmed as the pack of hounds came into view along the country lane. Looking down, he realized he still had his bag of aniseed with him, but it was too late, as the hounds poured into the village inn and tore him and several other customers to shreds.

May I add, as a footnote to this story, that hunt saboteurs were often known to use dried and preserved herrings to lay a trail in order to confuse foxhounds. Smoked or dried herring turns red in colour and this is the origin of the expression 'red herring', meaning 'false clue'.

Car Snooker

Police in Newcastle were unable to understand a recent sudden increase in thefts of cars, especially red ones. Deciding to set a trap, they left a cheap red car and an expensive white one in a vulnerable location at a city shopping precinct and settled down to observe them for the night. Before long, the surveillance officers noticed two men drive up and look around the car park. Ignoring the valuable white car, the thieves broke into the red one and started to drive off. Police officers soon surrounded the men and they were taken in for questioning. They later admitted they had been playing car snooker and the game meant one of them had to steal a red car before a black or blue one and then back to a red one again as the other 'player' totalled up the points. They claimed they were bored and it helped to pass the time. One of them even had a break going of fifty-four.

In 1999, the BBC reported that police in Devon and Cornwall were investigating a report of games of motorway snooker being played between officers on patrol. The rules were easy. Cops would stop speeding cars and score each one according to its colour as though it were a snooker ball: a red Peugeot would score one point, for instance, while a black Jeep would score seven. The highest break of the shift won.

Some claims were made that the number of points a licence was endorsed by also enhanced scores.

Naturally Devon and Cornwall police denied any wrongdoing by its officers but were forced to act when a motorist was stopped in a black Alfa Romeo on the M5. He told *The Times* he had asked officers why they had ignored a yellow Mini travelling at exactly the same speed as himself and was told about the motorway snooker games being played by patrol units. Devon and Cornwall police then issued a statement to the effect that people are stopped solely for speeding and that the colour of their car is irrelevant. But I don't believe them, and nor should you. So, top tips then:

1. Don't break the speed limit.
2. Don't drive a red car. There are fifteen red balls on a snooker table, making you fifteen times more likely to get stopped.
3. If you are driving a black car and see a red car being pulled over, slow down: you're next.
4. Don't drive a pink car. For one thing, they are worth six points, and for another you will look like an idiot.
5. You could drive a yellow car as they are worth only two points and rarely targeted, but they still don't look very good, do they?
6. The same goes for brown cars.
7. British racing green looks great and is worth

only three points, so go for a car painted green.

8. Or go for a white car. That's the cue ball and it is not supposed to be potted. Why do you think the police drive white cars? There you go – it must be true!

Free Tickets

A disgruntled Arsenal fan, disappointed with the club's recent performance, decided he did not want to go to the game the following weekend. With that, he left his match tickets clearly visible on the dashboard of his car, fully expecting them to be stolen. But on his return, he found four other tickets, presumably left by equally unhappy fans, had joined them.

Unnecessary Rescue

In 1988, two Scottish men had replied to a local newspaper advertisement offering a surplus naval life raft for sale. They felt the craft would be ideal for their fishing trips to the tranquil Scottish lochs, especially as the protective canopy fitted to all life rafts would be useful during the rain. As they began their first fishing trip using the raft, it started raining and the men settled in with flasks of hot tea while drifting across the silent loch waiting for a catch. But within minutes their peace was shattered by the sound of a naval helicopter hovering overhead and they began to curse the navy and their routine manoeuvres in the area. Their discomfort turned to panic, however, as they realized the zip to their canopy was being opened, from the outside, hundreds of yards from the nearest bit of shore. They huddled together in terror as a naval rescue operative and military doctor climbed into their raft. It soon became apparent the raft had been stolen from navy supplies and as soon as it had inflated the homing beacon was activated. Within minutes, rescue teams had been alerted on the assumption an accident had taken place.

The Lottery Loser

A man in a Midlands pub realized he had won £5 million on that evening's National Lottery draw. Amid huge celebrations the ticket was passed around the group of friends for proof of the win before finally being returned to the lucky winner. However, despite the ticket remaining in view the whole time, when it returned to its owner the numbers had changed. It had clearly been switched. While this is one of those stories that could easily be true, albeit unlikely, the same story has been told since the 1930s about a horseracing gambler who had just won a huge amount on the Grand National. In his case the betting slip returned to him had the name of a different racehorse written on it.

TRAVELLERS' TALES

The Missing Kidney

This is a story many people around the world believe to be true. It has been set in many different parts of the world – Turkey, Australia, South America, Eastern Europe – and in a number of different locations, such as nightclubs, strip clubs, restaurants or hotels. In fact, in the world

of urban legends it is something of an old chestnut. Once it was even released as an official warning to staff at an international company, going something like this:

We wish to warn all employees about a crime ring that is targeting business travellers. The criminals are ruthless, well organized, well funded and highly skilled, and they operate in many major cities around the world, most recently in Warsaw, Poland. The crime takes place when a business traveller relaxes in the lounge bar of their hotel and is approached and joined by another seemingly respectable businessman or lady. At some point a sedative is added to the traveller's drink and the next thing he (or she) knows is that he is waking up in a hotel bedroom in a bath full of iced water. There will be a note taped to the wall and telephone left nearby. The note warns the traveller not to move but to phone for an ambulance immediately. The traveller will then discover that an important body organ such as a kidney has been removed, stolen by a specialist surgeon – who will have set up a makeshift operating theatre in the hotel room – and then sold it on to a major hospital for transplant. Will all employees please be vigilant when travelling to foreign cities and never accept drinks from strangers.

This story has been reported as true since the mid 1990s, with many newspapers around the world printing similar warnings, but although there is little or no evidence confirming that any such muggings have actually taken place, it is fair to say that, if the human mind can imagine a particular activity, then someone, somewhere is probably doing it right at this moment.

However, what is well documented is the flourishing sale in body organs from poor countries, especially in Nepal. In the village of Hokse in the Kavre district, for instance, only fifty miles from Kathmandu, it has been reported that as many as seventy-five locals have sold a kidney for up to 60,000 rupees each, equivalent to around £750 and representing a small fortune for them. There have also been reports in some of the world's poorer countries of people agreeing to give blood for a fee, only to find out later they had a kidney removed in the process. While it is easy to dismiss such stories as fantasy, just remember this. It could happen!

And it could happen in even more sinister circumstances. After all, the *Moscow News*, on 25 October 2005, reported that a woman had been jailed for six years for selling her own daughter's vital organs. The news agency claimed that an official statement posted on the Russian Prosecutor General's Office website announced that Olga Zelentsova had been found guilty of human trafficking of a minor, committed with the intent of the victim's exploitation or withdrawal of the victim's organs or tissues. The court had found that the alcoholic and unemployed mother had attempted to sell her own six-year-old daughter for US$10,000 to an undercover police officer acting as a potential customer. The woman had been told the child would be sexually abused and then probably used as a donor for body parts.

Vibrating Baggage

A married couple were sitting on a plane at Dallas airport in Texas when the lady's name was called out over the public address system. She was asked to get off the plane and speak to security staff who were concerned about her baggage, currently being loaded into the hold. Out on the runway, officials told her there was something 'suspicious' vibrating in her suitcase. The lady assured the men this must be the 'adult' toy the couple had bought during their trip, which neither she nor her husband realized was sold with batteries already fitted.

Unconvinced, the security officials asked the lady to open her suitcase and identify the item, which she did, exposing to the full view – and vast amusement – of the passengers along one side of the plane a still-quivering vibrator. Once the batteries had been removed, she was allowed to repack her new 'toy' and continue her journey home.

The woman later filed a lawsuit against Delta

Airlines, citing humiliation and loss of dignity, and claiming security officials had made 'obnoxious and embarrassing comments' to her during the ordeal. She rapidly became the subject of talk-show jokes all over America. This is, in fact, a true story and the names of those involved are well documented. I am tempted to reveal them . . . but hasn't she suffered enough already?

Body in the Bed

A young couple had booked into a Florida hotel to begin their honeymoon but, on reaching their suite, noticed an unpleasant smell. The man telephoned reception and complained about the problem, asking whether they could move to a new room, only to be told by the reservations manager that the hotel was fully booked for the evening due to a large business conference being held in one of the convention suites. The manager, however, apologized for the inconvenience and offered the couple a complimentary lunch for two, with wine, in the exclusive à la carte restaurant. He assured the couple he would send the cleaners to attend to the problem while they were having lunch and the problem would be resolved by the time they returned.

After a fine meal they returned to the room, but the unpleasant odour still lingered in the air, so they once again approached reception, demanding to see the manager in person. This time the manager tried to find them a room in another hotel but found them all booked up for the next two days. He suggested the couple take advantage of the hotel's local tour guide for the afternoon, followed up by dinner in the same restaurant, once again complimentary, and an evening in the casino with free gambling tokens.

The contract cleaners attended to the room but once again, as nobody could deny, the smell continued to linger. Staff had searched the entire room, changing sheets, towels and curtains, even washing the carpets, and still could not trace the source of the smell. Upon returning in the small hours, the young man became angry and began to tear the room apart. As he heaved the mattress from the base of the bed, his young wife screamed in horror. Before her lay the decomposing body of a woman. Who she was and how she got there remain a mystery to this day.

The Bride Who Disappeared

This 'body in the hotel' legend has similarities with another story concerning a young married couple. In the summer of 1975, two youngsters, each only eighteen years old, decided to get married. The bride's father, a successful business-man living in a mansion in Palm Beach, was able to provide a beautiful and expensive reception for the couple at an exclusive local hotel. The wedding went ahead as planned and they were married on the terrace overlooking the sea. As the reception drew to a close, the couple and their friends stayed up drinking as the older guests retired for the night. The drinking games became more adventurous until somebody suggested a game of hide and seek around the rambling hotel. Everyone agreed and the groom set about finding his friends, locating all of them one by one, until only one person was missing – his new bride. After hours of searching, the party guests became angry with the bride and, believing she was playing a bad trick on them, gave up looking and went to bed. Eventually so did the bridegroom.

A subsequent search the following day failed to trace the girl and so the police were called. Officers took the missing person report with a pinch of salt and advised the family that it was not unknown for youngsters to change their minds about marrying so young and to take flight. Both the groom and the bride's family were heartbroken but as the days turned into weeks, weeks into months and eventually years, the young man tried to get on with his life, although always on the lookout for his bride, believing she would return to him one day. Then, three years later, during routine maintenance on the hotel, workmen discovered a huge old trunk in the corner of the attic. Dusting it down and opening it revealed the body of the young bride. The police investigation showed she had attempted to hide in the trunk but the lid had knocked her temporarily unconscious and the lock had clicked into place as it fell. She had hidden herself too well and nobody had thought to look for her up in the attic.

This story is in fact based upon a much older legend, the subject of a popular ballad called 'The Mistletoe Bough' written by Thomas Haynes (1797–1839). It is set at Christmas in a castle hall hung with mistletoe and holly. The company is 'blithe and gay' but the baron's beautiful daughter, 'young Lovell's bride', grows tired of the dancing and runs off to play hide and seek. Her friends and lover search for her, but in vain; she cannot be found. The years roll by until:

> At length an oak chest that had long lain hid
> Was found in the castle. They raised the lid,
> And a skeleton form lay mouldering there,
> In the bridal wreath of the lady fair.

Because of the enormous popularity of the song, several English stately homes claimed to be the castle in the story. And they do to this day, at Minster Lovell in Oxfordshire, at Bramshill House and Marwell Old Hall, both in Hampshire, and at Brockdish Hall in Norfolk.

Caught with Her Pants Down

The skiing accident story seems to be told by people every year as they return from the slopes. The late Jeffrey Bernard in his *Spectator* column once recalled it, and it has even been reported as true by one American newspaper. According to the tale, a young lady, halfway through a skiing holiday, found herself badly needing the bathroom. As there was clearly none to be found up there on the mountain, she decided to conceal herself behind a large tree and let nature take its course. Sadly, however, she had her skis pointing downhill and, crouching with her salopettes around her knees, she took off at high speed. Her embarrassment was compounded when the young lady realized she was heading directly for a large group standing at the bottom of the slope waiting for the ski lift. As luck would have it, she was the only one to be injured in the ensuing pile-up, which left her with a broken leg and ice burns on her backside.

Later, as the medical helicopter was about to take her to hospital, a young man with a broken arm joined her and she asked him how he had hurt himself. The man explained that he had been on the ski lift when a crazy girl flew past him at high speed with her trousers around her ankles, and he had shifted in his seat to get a better view, falling off and breaking his arm in the process. Then he asked her what had happened to her.

I'd like to think they fell in love, got married and lived happily ever after. What a way to meet if they did.

The Biscuit Snatcher

This frequently recounted tale has even been told on Radio 4, with one listener phoning in to claim it actually happened to her husband. It goes like this. A city gentleman takes his seat on the train at one of the tables and puts his newspaper, coffee and packet of biscuits down in front of him. He is then joined by an unruly-looking youth with regulation rucksack and spiky hair, almost wearing his jeans. A short while into the journey, the youth rummages around in his rucksack, then leans forward, opens the packet of biscuits and eats one of them. The man is amazed but does not want to create a scene. Instead, he reaches for the packet, takes out two and eats them. The youth stares at him and does the same thing himself. This goes on with the two of them eating the biscuits and all the while staring at each other. As the train pulls into the next station, the man, in a fit of temper, smashes his fist into the packet, reducing the biscuits to crumbs, then tells the youth he can finish them now, before getting up to leave.

However, as he picks up his newspaper, he notices his own unopened packet of biscuits hiding underneath. The ones he had been eating belonged to the spiky-haired youth. Now, as with all legends and tall tales, this could easily have happened, and it probably has. But I have read or heard many different versions of this story, with cigarettes, mints and chewing gum instead of biscuits, and a boat or aeroplane instead of a train. Jeffrey Archer even made a short story out of it called 'The Broken Routine', published in 1980 in *A Quiver Full of Arrows*.

Don't Touch that Button

During the 1970s, an aircraft went missing over the Gulf of Mexico and it was soon discovered the plane had crashed into the sea without warning, killing all eighty-five people on board. No radio alerts had been issued by the pilots and there was no obvious reason for the accident. Investigators were sent to the scene and soon located the wreckage of the stricken plane, including the black box holding all recorded flight data. Listening later to the recordings of the flight crew, they heard the co-pilot say, 'I wonder what happens if you push this button?' The recording ends there – this was the last thing anybody said. Investigators have still to ascertain which button was pressed.

The Clam Handcuffs

A man had taken a diving holiday to Madagascar, in the Indian Ocean, and was enjoying the crystal-clear, warm sea and all the marine life around him. On one of his dives, he noticed an underwater cave and, as he got closer, saw a giant clam clinging to the rock face, its two valves open wide. Realizing how much a clam of that size would be worth, he approached it with his diving knife. Holding the knife in one hand, he held on to both halves of the giant clam and began to prise them away from the surface, but the clam slammed shut, trapping his hand firmly. He tried in vain to force the clam open but all attempts failed and he soon realized he was running out of oxygen. Knowing he had only one chance of escape, he started sawing away at his own wrist, eventually cutting his hand off to free himself and rising to the surface just as his oxygen supply ran out. Later, rescue teams located the clam, but its valves were open again and there was no sign of the hand, which had probably made a tasty meal for some passing fish.

This story may or may not be true but it reminds us of a lone hiker called Aaron Ralston who became trapped in a canyon at Grand Junction in Colorado in 2003. While squeezing through a three-foot-wide slot canyon, a one-ton boulder slipped and pinned him by the arm. Unable to move, Ralston was trapped for five days and, realizing his chances of survival were rapidly diminishing, took the agonizing decision to cut off his own arm with a pocket knife. He then applied a tourniquet, climbed out of the canyon and walked to safety. Also in Colorado, in October 1993, a lone fisherman called Bill

Jeracki became trapped by a boulder, which fell on his leg while he was fishing in a remote mountain region. With a snowstorm forecast for that evening and wearing only light clothing, Jeracki feared he would not survive the night. Knowing he had little choice, he cut off his leg at the knee using a fishing knife, crawled half a mile to his truck and drove himself to hospital. Both remarkable stories, and both true.

Exploding Breasts

A story that has been circulating for decades warning of the perils of flying was first reported in the *Reader's Digest* in 1958. The story claimed that the sales manager of an inflatable-bra company was flying between Los Angeles and San Francisco with one of his lingerie models. Naturally enough she was wearing one of the company's products but neither of them realized the effects cabin pressure at altitude would have on the bra. The higher the plane went, the larger her breasts became and she eventually had to take refuge in the cockpit until the aircraft's descent reduced them to a less conspicuous size. Mammoth-breasted models on the flight deck were obviously no distraction for the plucky pilots as the plane landed quite safely.

But as bosom-enhancing technology has improved over the years, so the story has changed and now it is quite common to hear an account of a famous actress or model who finds her silicone breast implants swelling up on long-haul flights, even though extensive tests have revealed cabin pressures between 8,000 and 30,000 feet above sea level have no adverse effect on breast implants. So much for in-flight entertainment, then. Tests have revealed no change occurs in deep-sea situations either. So there you are, ladies: you can all go for a ride in a submarine without your breasts exploding, which must be a relief to know.

Things that Go Bump in the Night

An English couple, travelling to Moscow for the first time, had arrived at their hotel late at night. After checking in and being shown to their room, they decided to order a meal using room service and then settle down to watch *Sky News*. As the man walked across the room, he noticed a strange lump in the carpet, which on further inspection turned out to be a metal plate screwed into the floor. After removing the screws and plate so as not to trip on them during the night, he then retired to bed. The following morning the receptionist asked if the couple had slept well and they replied that they had. 'That's good,' continued the receptionist, 'because in the middle of the night the chandelier fell on the couple in the room below you.'

This story has been told many times over the years, with the couple being replaced by different people, such as an American diplomat or members of a football team, and the idea was even used in one of the most famous scenes in the English TV comedy series *Only Fools and Horses* during the 1980s, in the appropriately named episode 'A Touch of Glass'. As long ago as 1972 it was being told about an ice hockey team from Canada visiting Moscow for a match.

Crime Doesn't Pay

Deep in the middle of the Australian outback a traveller realized he was running low on petrol and, as it was late in the evening, was starting to worry. A few miles along the road, he noticed a campsite and thought he would be able to find petrol there so he pulled up and, taking his can with him, walked through the gates and approached the main office. But there was no sign of life there or in any of the caravans, as everybody appeared to be sleeping peacefully. Realizing he had little option, the traveller decided to steal some petrol by siphoning a canful from one of the larger camper vans, so he took out a tube, opened one of the tanks and began to suck. He knew the petrol would taste foul, but wasn't expecting to be violently sick – as he was when it dawned on him that he'd opened the wrong tank and was siphoning the waste from a chemical toilet.

The Terminal Man

Mehran Karimi Nasseri, also known as Sir Alfred Mehran, is an Iranian refugee who claims to be the son of an Iranian doctor and an English nurse. He says he was born on the Anglo-Persian Oil Company compound in Masjed Soleiman, Iran, where his father was working at the time. He arrived in England in 1973 to take a three-year course in Yugoslav studies at Bradford University, during which time he became involved in a protest movement against the Shah of Iran. However, in 1974 his university grant was suddenly revoked and he was returned to Tehran where he was promptly arrested at the airport and taken to Evin prison by SAVAK, the Iranian secret police. There he was tortured for four months before being expelled from his homeland. He spent the next six years wandering Europe applying for political asylum, which was refused by West Germany and Holland (1977), France (1978), Yugoslavia and Italy (1979), France again and Britain (1980), before he was finally accepted into Belgium in late 1980 – having been granted asylum by the United Nations High Commission for Refugees – where he lived until 1988. Having decided at this point to move to England, Nasseri then lost his papers, claiming he had been mugged while waiting for his flight at the Charles de Gaulle airport, and as he was unable to prove his identity or refugee status, he was taken to a holding zone for travellers without papers. He remained there, at the airport, for four years before his case was taken up by the human-rights lawyer Christian Bourget. In 1992, the French court ruled he could not legally be forced to leave the country. But they also refused him a French visa so he was unable to leave the holding zone of the airport either, and there he remains, to this day, living at Charles de Gaulle airport, where he has become something of a fixture and fitting.

He wakes up at 5 a.m. every morning and washes in the public toilets before spending his day around the terminal reading books donated by travellers, listening to the radio and writing his diary. Sympathetic airport staff often wash his clothes for him and have even supplied him with an old sofa for his comfort. His diaries have been turned into a book called *The Terminal Man*, published in 2004, which has been described by the *Sunday Times* as 'profoundly disturbing and brilliant'.

In 1999, the French court finally granted Nasseri a temporary residential permit and provided a refugee passport which would have allowed him to leave the airport and live in France, but the Iranian's failing mental health was apparent when he refused to sign the papers, claiming they did not identify him properly. So, at the time of writing, there at the airport he remains, lost in transit, having lived in the terminal for eighteen long years, to all appearances just a traveller waiting in the departure lounge with his possessions in a bag beside him. His vagrant lifestyle belies the fact that he is in fact a wealthy man, ever since Steven Spielberg's DreamWorks Company paid a reported US$250,000 for the film rights to his life, which is said to be the inspiration behind the 2004 film *The Terminal* starring Tom Hanks and Catherine Zeta Jones.

THE AMERICAN PRESIDENCY

Our President, the Idiot

Tom Bihn is a small manufacturer of bags based in Port Angeles, Washington. Its products are sold in both the US and Canada and consequently the cleaning instructions on each label are produced in both English and French. Apparently a joke between a seamstress and company staff led to the words 'Nous sommes desolés que notre president soit un idiot. Nous n'avons pas voté pour lui' being added to the French washing instructions, which went unnoticed until the consignment of bags arrived in Canada and French-speaking shop staff read the new instructions, which can be translated as:

Wash with warm water.
Use mild soap.
Dry flat.
Do not bleach.
Do not machine dry.
Do not iron.

We are sorry that our President is an idiot.
We did not vote for him.

What started as an urban legend, however, turns out to be true, as the company's website explains: 'The "secret" message began as an inside joke among seamstresses and staff at the Tom Bihn factory and was apparently intended to poke fun at company's founder and president, Tom Bihn.' Tom Bihn himself, maybe wisely, is sticking to this interpretation. 'I'm going with the idea that it's a joke about me,' he told the Associated Press, then added: 'Clearly when you use the word "idiot" and "president" in the same sentence, many people will jump to other conclusions . . .'

The Tom Bihn company has found its sales rocketing all over North America since the new label was produced.

Presidential Coincidences

Abraham Lincoln was elected to the US Congress in 1846.

John F. Kennedy was elected to the US Congress in 1946.

Abraham Lincoln was elected President in 1861.

John F. Kennedy was elected President in 1961.

Their surnames each contain seven letters.

Both of them were particularly concerned with the civil rights issue.

Both their wives lost a child while living in the White House.

Lincoln and Kennedy were shot on a Friday.

Both presidents were shot in the back of the head.

Lincoln's secretary was called Kennedy.

Kennedy's secretary was called Lincoln.

Southerners assassinated both presidents.

They were both succeeded by Southerners.

Lincoln was succeeded by Andrew Johnson.

Kennedy was succeeded by Lyndon Johnson.

Andrew Johnson was born in 1808.

Lyndon Johnson was born in 1908.

Andrew Johnson was President until 1869.

Lyndon Johnson was President until 1969.

John Wilkes Booth, who assassinated Lincoln, was born in 1839.

Lee Harvey Oswald, who assassinated Kennedy, was born in 1939.

Both assassins were known by their full three names.

Both names comprise fifteen letters.

Booth ran from the theatre and was caught in a warehouse.

Oswald ran from a warehouse and was caught in a theatre.

Booth and Oswald were both assassinated before their trials.

The President's Brain is Missing

Everyone of a certain age, the world over, knows that the thirty-fifth President of the United States, John F. Kennedy, was shot and fatally wounded on Friday, 22 November 1963. He was riding through Dealey Plaza in Dallas, Texas, in the presidential motorcade at the time and the assassination was captured live on a few home movies, notably the one made by amateur cameraman Abraham Zapruder which provided the famous clips most of us have seen and is known throughout the world as the Zapruder Film. The following days provided endless news coverage, the like of which was not to be seen again – until the terrorist attacks on New York and Washington on 11 September 2001. This coverage led to the many conspiracy theories that have been debated and argued about ever since, with films, documentaries and books all offering their various opinions.

The main point of debate is that the official version of events concluded Kennedy was shot from behind by a lone gunman, Lee Harvey Oswald, from an upstairs window of the Texas School Book Depository, while the Zapruder Film clearly shows Kennedy's head slam backwards and to the left, defying the laws of physics if the official conclusion is to be believed – which is why not many people do believe it. This has

given rise to the widely held theory there was more than one gunman, and the famous 'Grassy Knoll' has emerged as the most likely location from where the fatal shots were fired. No bullets were found to confirm the presence of a second gunman, leading to the 'ice bullet' theory (see 'Ice Bullets'), but needless to say this did not put off the conspiracy theorists and many doctors were also not satisfied at the time.

But there would have been an easy way to resolve matters and to determine the direction the fatal shots were fired in that would have forestalled decades of fruitless debate. In any case of death by gunshot to the head, the standard procedure would be for a forensic expert to examine the brain of the victim and to study detailed X-rays of tissue samples which would determine how many shots had been fired and from which direction – front, rear or side. But this was never done for the American President, or at least the findings were never publicly released. After Kennedy had been shot, he was taken directly to Trauma Room One of the Parkland Memorial Hospital where he was officially pronounced dead at 1.38 p.m. A tense confrontation then followed between doctors, local officials and armed secret service agents, who then drew their weapons and removed the President's body at 2 p.m. before it could undergo a forensic examination by the Dallas coroner. This action was against Texas state law and as, at that time, it was not a federal offence to kill the President, the state law should have prevailed and the body been retained for examination. Kennedy was then taken to the Andrews air base in Washington DC, which was when all the conflicting opinions began to emerge.

In Dallas, doctors claimed the President had sustained wounds to the front of his head, while in Washington the official autopsy stated the point of entry was to the back of the head. The mortician who reassembled the President's skull for burial claimed he found a bullet wound to Kennedy's right temple. All officials needed to do to verify which of the conflicting claims was true was to examine the President's brain. The problem was that when Kennedy's body arrived at Bethesda Naval Hospital in Washington DC, a naval medical technician, as he later testified on oath, found the President's cranial cavity to be completely empty – his brain had been removed, presumably en route between Dallas and Washington. And so all the conspiracy theorists and urban legend fans who claim the President's brain is missing are in fact correct. Now, I can think of subsequent presidents whose brains *appear* to be missing, but in Kennedy's case it was true, and it remains missing to this day. In 1998, the *Washington Post* revealed Kennedy's personal physician, the late Admiral George Burkley, had left the hospital with the president's brain, stating that he was going to 'deliver it to the Attorney General [Robert Kennedy]', as lab technician John T. Stringer is reported to have noted, 'presumably for burial'. Although unsubstantiated, this seems the likeliest explanation.

While we are on the subject of the Kennedys, we should consider another myth surrounding one of their clan, in this case JFK's younger brother Robert. Bobby Kennedy served with distinction as Attorney General during his brother's administration and was widely regarded as the more talented of the two. Many people believed he was on the verge of making history on the night of 5 June 1968 when he accepted the Californian nomination to become the Democratic presidential candidate at the Ambassador Hotel in Los Angeles. The only problem was that as he was leaving to the cheers of his supporters, he was shot dead by a 24-year-old Palestinian immigrant, Sirhan B. Sirhan, or at least that is the official verson of events. The truth is that while Sirhan did appear a few yards in front of Kennedy and fired eight shots from his handgun, ten bullets were later accounted for, leading to speculation that Sirhan may have been firing blanks and two other gunmen were present. Dr Thomas T. Noguchi, a world-famous pathologist, testified on oath that the bullet which killed Bobby Kennedy had entered his head behind his right ear, having been fired from a distance of between one and three inches. Indeed, Noguchi recorded thick powder burns on Kennedy's skin as well as two other bullet entry points at the top and back of his right shoulder. He always remained cautious and diplomatic when commenting on his findings and noted in his biography *Coroner*, published a decade after the shooting: 'Until more is precisely known, the existence of a second gunman remains a possibility. Thus, I have never said that Sirhan Sirhan killed Robert Kennedy.'

In addition, no single witness report ever revealed Sirhan to have been any closer to Kennedy than five or six feet away, and at no time was he behind him. The only person who appears to have been in such a position was a private security guard called Thane Eugene Cesar, who was walking to the right of Kennedy, holding on to his right elbow. He was also in possession of a .22 pistol of the kind that had fired the bullets in question but, when confronted with the evidence, stated he had sold the pistol before the assassination. However, after witnesses testified he had been seen drawing his handgun and that it was later observed to be 'smoking', he then changed his story, claiming that he did have the pistol with him on the night of the attack but had sold it soon afterwards. Investigators tracked down the new owner in Arkansas but were told the gun had been stolen and consequently no forensic examination has ever been made of the weapon.

Cesar was also a known opponent of the John Kennedy administration, but he did agree to undergo a polygraph (lie detector) test and remained open about his political leanings. He was also not originally scheduled for duty that evening and had been called in as a last-minute replacement, which would have left him no time to plan properly such a high-profile political assassination. Hence, despite being caught in the crossfire of history (if you'll excuse the pun) Cesar has never been much more than a simple curiosity to many observers, and as Cesar himself has once said: 'Just because I don't like Democrats doesn't mean I go round shooting them.'

To this day, Sirhan Sirhan and his family still plead his innocence. I draw no conclusion but I note the comment in the pathologist's official report that Sirhan could not have killed Bobby Kennedy.

LOOK BEHIND YOU!

Granny in the Back Seat

From North Wales comes the story of a young woman who returned to her car, parked in the local multi-storey car park, to find an elderly lady sitting in the back seat. As it was a popular make of car, she first checked the number plate and, assured it was indeed her vehicle, asked the lady what she was doing there. The old lady explained she had been shopping with her daughter and grandchildren but had felt unwell and wanted to return to the car for a rest. She explained her daughter's car was the same make, model and colour as the young woman's and she must have got into the wrong one – a plausible enough explanation. The old lady then began to breathe heavily and, holding her chest, asked to be taken to the local hospital, which the driver agreed to do. But just as the young woman was about to reverse out of the parking space, she noticed in the rearview mirror that the old lady's shawl had slipped, revealing a muscular arm,

thick with hair. Worried about the situation she had placed herself in, the young woman asked the old lady to direct her out of the parking space by standing to one side of the bay and was relieved when she agreed to do this. Once out of the parking bay, the young woman locked the doors and sped off to the nearest police station to report the matter. Police officers then searched the car, finding a rope and an axe under the passenger seat. The young woman had had a fortunate escape, although the situation would not have arisen in the first place if she had remembered to lock her car up before she went shopping.

Psycho Drama

In a similar vein to the previous tale, a story is often told of a girl who had spent the evening out with a group of friends and was driving home, unaccompanied, late at night. Travelling along a deserted country lane, she noticed, glancing in her rearview mirror, a car approaching and preparing to overtake her. The car indicated and manoeuvred as if to pass, then quickly swerved back in behind her and began flashing its headlights. It sat on the girl's tail for a number of miles, its lights flashing and the driver gesticulating madly all the while. Naturally frightened, the girl accelerated and drove into the nearest town. Seeing a busy petrol station, she swerved on to the forecourt, screeched to a halt and jumped out of the car. The driver of the following car did the same and screamed at her to lock the door, explaining he had already called the police, who then arrived in a matter of seconds. The grisly truth was soon revealed when the man explained that he had been about to overtake her when he noticed the silhouette of a man on her back seat with a large knife in his hand. When he had seen the flash of lights, the shadowy figure had crouched back down and remained hidden for the rest of the journey. Opening the back door of the car, the police discovered a dangerous lunatic hiding behind the driver's seat.

Never Give Lifts to Strangers

Another oft-repeated urban tale involving a lady driver takes us to Denver in America and the Cherry Creek Shopping Center. One day, during late autumn, a woman returned to her car with a week's shopping in bags to find she had a flat tyre. Unused to dealing with such mechanical matters, the woman was at a loss. As luck would have it, a handsome middle-aged man dressed in a smart business suit approached and offered to help. Full of gratitude, she watched as he unloaded the boot of her car, jacked it up and replaced the punctured tyre with the spare. He then loaded the boot back up with the tools and the bags of shopping and explained to the lady where the nearest puncture repair centre was, insisting she should go straight there as another puncture would leave her stranded. With that, he asked the lady for a lift around to the other side of the shopping centre, where his own car was parked very close to the exit.

Feeling a little uncomfortable about this, although not wanting to appear ungrateful after he had been so helpful, she hesitated, asking him why he was on this side of the parking lot, if his own car was so far away. The man explained he had just walked his elderly mother safely back to her own car when he spotted the 'lady in distress'. Still not convinced, the woman claimed she had left something in the shopping centre that she had to go and collect, but that she would give him a lift on her return. Once back at the centre, she explained to the security guard what had happened. He immediately agreed to return to the car with her, just to be on the safe side. Once there, they found the man was nowhere to be seen, but that his executive briefcase had been left in the boot. The guard opened it and found inside a length of rope, some handcuffs, a gag and a large butcher's knife. When later she took the damaged tyre to the repair centre, she was told there was nothing wrong with it at all, and that the air had simply been let out. A close shave indeed.

Babysitting Nightmare

One evening, in a remote village deep in the North Yorkshire moors, Lucy turned up for her regular job babysitting two young children. She arrived at around 5 p.m., made supper, played with the children and helped finish off some of their homework before putting them both to bed at 8 p.m. As usual, the parents weren't expected home until very late. As the dark winter evening drew in, she settled down in front of the television – just as the phone rang.

There was a man on the other end of the line. 'At midnight,' the voice said, 'I am going to come and kill you.' Lucy immediately hung up and, very shaken, immediately phoned her family and boyfriend, who reassured her it was probably a random call from some crank. Settling back down again, she forgot all about the call until the phone rang again. Expecting it to be her family checking on her, she answered immediately.

'Hello again,' said the voice. 'It is getting closer now and at midnight I am coming for you.' The line went dead. Lucy hurried upstairs to check on the children. They were sleeping peacefully and everything seemed normal, but it didn't stop her checking all the door locks and double-bolting the windows.

An hour later, at around 11 p.m., the phone rang again. 'Hello, my dear, nearly time ...' came the voice, before the line went dead again. This time Lucy telephoned the police. After she had explained what had happened, the police operator told her they would put a trace on the line. If the man phoned again, she was to try and keep him talking so they could establish the location from which the call was being made.

Within half an hour, the phone rang once again: 'Hello, sweetheart, it's nearly time for us to meet. I hope you are looking forward to it.' This time Lucy tried to keep the caller on the line. 'Who are you?' she asked. 'Why are you doing this?' But the sinister voice just repeated, 'I am coming to see you and the children soon. Will you leave the door open for me?' Still clutching the phone, Lucy panicked and raced to the front door to check it was bolted. She could hear menacing laughter down the line and screamed, 'Who are you, why are you doing this to me?' 'Just make sure you are ready for me, darling,' said the voice, and the line went dead.

Shortly before midnight, Lucy heard cars pull

up along the lane and hurried footsteps outside. There was a knock on the door and a man's voice was calling her name. By now she was frozen with terror. She screamed as the old cottage door burst off its hinges and shadowy figures poured into the hallway, some racing up the stairs, some to the back of the house, while two came towards her, as she crouched behind the settee in the living room. 'Lucy,' a female voice called. 'It's all right, you're safe now.' Disorientated, Lucy tried to focus through her tears and finally made out the uniforms of two female police officers trying to calm her. Behind them, armed officers carried the children down the stairs and outside to safety and a scuffle was heard in the room overhead. 'What's happening?' Lucy cried. 'We traced the calls,' one of the officers told her. 'They were coming from a separate telephone line inside the house.'

The Famous Hook Story

A teenage couple had been out on a first date to the cinema in a remote town in western France and had bought some burgers to eat on the journey home. Pulling over into a deserted but well-known lovers' lane, they ate the food and, after throwing the papers into a nearby dustbin, the lad returned to the car, feeling he was about to get lucky. He turned on the radio and

the pair began kissing and cuddling before a news flash interrupted the song that was playing. They both listened as the radio presenter gave a warning that a convicted mass murderer had escaped from a nearby mental hospital and advised listeners not to approach the man under any circumstances. A description was given, including the man's height, hair colour and clothing and the fact he had a hook in place of his right hand, an obvious distinguishing feature. The girl began to feel a little uneasy but the lad, not wanting his evening to be spoilt, simply locked the doors and assured the girl they would be safe. But the girl was still frightened and, pushing the lad off her, insisted on being driven home. Frustrated and fed up, the youth slammed the car into gear and sped out of the layby, the wheels of his car spinning. The two didn't speak on the journey home, but as he dropped the girl off, she began screaming uncontrollably as she stepped out of the car. Alarmed, he raced round to her side of the car as neighbours also ran out to investigate. There, attached to the door handle and dripping blood, was the hooked hand. Evidence that the monster had been moments from reaching her back in lovers' lane.

Don't Look Back

In a very similar tale to the previous one, a young couple had driven to a secluded area for a little in-car passion under the stars. Listening to the radio, they discovered that a dangerous inmate of a local lunatic asylum had escaped and a full-scale manhunt was now underway. The couple decided to drive to a safer area on the other side of town but the car refused to start so the young man had no choice other than run for help. He told his girlfriend not to get out of the car under any circumstances and to keep the doors locked. With that he disappeared into the darkness. As the night drew on, the terrified girl huddled under her blanket and was scared of every noise, even the scratching sound she could hear on the roof of the car, which was probably just the leaves of an overhanging tree gently brushing the vehicle. The boy never returned, but as dawn broke she saw the flashing blue light of a police car heading towards her and began to feel safe for the first time. Officers approached her car and ordered her out, instructing her not to look behind her at any point. Naturally the girl looked back, only to see the headless body of her boyfriend hanging upside down from a tree with his fingernails scraping gently across the roof of the car.

Don't Turn the Light On

Here is a story that has been frightening college students for decades, once again often with somebody claiming it actually happened to a person they knew.

A girl was working alone in a college library. It was getting late and, realizing that she was probably going to have to stay there all night, she decided to go back to her room and pick up a jumper. As she walked back across the deserted campus, she could see that her window was dark and assumed her roommate must be asleep. She quietly opened the bedroom door and, hearing heavy breathing, she didn't turn on the light but swiftly crept in, grabbed her jumper and crept out again.

Dawn was breaking as she finished her essay and she decided to go back to her room to wash and get changed. But when she got back to her floor, she found three policemen standing outside her room. They told her that something terrible had happened. Her roommate had been found horribly murdered, and they needed her help deciphering a strange message they'd found just inside the room. So she took a deep breath and opened the door. And there on the wall, scrawled in her roommate's blood were the words: 'AREN'T YOU GLAD YOU DIDN'T TURN THE LIGHT ON?'

It is enough to give you nightmares, although not as bad as mine. Last night I dreamt Jordan (no, not the country) had won custody of me in the High Court. It was enough to have me fumbling around in the dark for the brandy bottle. When I slept again, I slept soundly, this time dreaming of escape.

Driving with the Lights Off

A story has been circulating in England since the 1990s about a gang of youths who cruise around in their car with the headlights off and chase the first car to flash its lights at them. If they are able to catch the driver, he is then subjected to a horrendous assault as part of an initiation ritual for a new gang member. The story has caused alarm and even been the subject of local newspaper items but, in fact, it is generally believed to be nothing more than an urban legend that has its origins in America, where certain gangs were alleged to use such an initiation ritual. Even over on that side of the pond, it is thought to be untrue, however. John Moore, a senior researcher at the National Youth Gang Centre, in an attempt to quash the persistent rumour, told the *Washington Post* that, to the best of his knowledge, the rumour was untrue. 'I know of no incident in the country where this type of thing occurred,' he told reporters. 'This is one of the wonders of the internet, that you can take something that has no basis in fact and make people believe it.' How true: it is easy to see why so many people get taken in by internet rumours, the veracity of a story growing the more frequently it is told, but, with no evidence to back it up, why fall for it in the first place? I don't.

The Graveyard Dare

A group of teenage girls were having a sleepover party one weekend in an isolated Lancashire village. Taking turns to tell each other tales of ghostly goings-on, one of the girls claimed an old man had been buried in the local graveyard the previous week and that he had been buried alive. She insisted that if they went to the grave, he could be heard trying to scratch his way out.

The other girls refused to believe this at first, but eventually they all agreed to go down to the churchyard together to find out. Naturally they were terrified and, on reaching the entrance to the graveyard, all of them lost their nerve except the girl who had told them the story in the first place. The others went back home to wait for their friend but, in the event, she never returned. The group assumed their friend had also lost her nerve but, not wishing to lose face, had herself gone home. That was until the following morning when they found her lying dead by the old man's grave. The subsequent police investigation revealed she had caught her nightdress on a nearby headstone and, unable to run, had died of shock.

Three Men and a Ghost

According to some observers, there are a number of scenes, during the popular film *Three Men and a Baby* starring Tom Selleck, where the ghost of a young boy, supposedly killed in the house where filming was taking place, appears in the background. At one point there appears to be a rifle pointing at the head of the ghost. But the facts do not lend any credibility to the legend.

For a start, the film was made in a Hollywood studio not, as often reported, a haunted house. Also, the ghostly shape is, in fact, the shadow of a cardboard cut-out of Selleck's co-star Ted Danson that had been left on set by a stagehand. The promotional cut-out can also be seen in full view in another scene during the film. The story that the parents of the dead boy later sued the film's producers for compensation for their distress is consequently untrue too. Indeed, there are no ghostly goings-on in *Three Men and a Baby*, apart from some of the performances, which should have been invisible to the naked eye.

The blockbuster movie *The Wizard of Oz* also features a shadowy figure, said to be that of a man who hanged himself from the branch of a tree, and who went unnoticed by the film crew, swinging in the background during one of the scenes. The truth, however, is less interesting. The 'hanging figure' is simply a crew member who found himself caught in the camera shot and who quickly ran off the set. The editor decided it was insignificant to the point of not wasting time and money to refilm the scene, initiating an enduring urban legend at a stroke.

Another enduring legend is that the actress who played the deceitful secretary in the James Bond classic *Goldfinger* actually died after the famous scene in which she is seen lying dead on the bed with her naked body painted gold.

This reflects the belief at the time that the human body breathes through the skin as well as the lungs, so that blocking all of the pores could cause death. As it happens, the film makers did have doctors standing by just in case the actress, Shirley Eaton, should succumb, but she remained healthy and made several more films before quietly retiring from the film industry.

The Ghost of Newstead Abbey

It was just after eleven on a cold, rainy night in January, when the last scheduled bus trundled along the A60 from Mansfield, heading back to Nottingham. As the driver neared Newstead Abbey, famously once the home of Lord Byron, the rain became heavier and, squinting into the darkness, he almost missed the lone gentleman standing at the bus shelter. The driver was surprised as it was unusual for anyone to catch a bus so late at night from this particular location, miles from anywhere. But the man boarded the bus and, without saying a word, made his way up the stairs to the top deck. The driver then pulled away and woke his conductor, asking him to deal with the fare. The conductor had neither seen nor heard the bus come to a halt, and hadn't noticed anyone climb on board, but he wearily made his way up the stairs. Clomping back down again, he seemed a little annoyed, accusing the driver of fooling with him, as there was nobody at all on the upper deck. The driver assured him there was and insisted he check again. This time, when the conductor returned, a full-scale argument broke out and the driver stopped the bus on a remote stretch of road directly outside Newstead Abbey.

At that moment, the man descended the stairs, calmly walked between them and stood waiting at the doors. The driver informed the man they were not at a bus stop but the gentleman neither replied nor turned around. The conductor at first looked on in stunned disbelief as the driver once again informed the passenger he could not get off the bus. But then, feeling a strange sensation take control of him, the conductor reached past the driver and operated the door control. With that, the man got off the bus and disappeared into the cold night, in the direction of the famous abbey.

Clubbers, Beware!

A young girl had been out partying with friends in London and, as usual, had a little too much to drink. Taking a taxi home in the early hours, she realized she had lost her handbag and immediately phoned the police. The following morning she cancelled her credit cards but then received a phone call from a man claiming to have found the bag. He said he had discovered it in the toilets of a club he worked at but did not want to hand it in to bar staff as he was sure the girl would never see it again if he did. He told her he was a DJ working at a recording studio in east London and asked her to meet him at a tube station later that day so he could return it to her personally. Being a cautious girl when sober, she took a friend along with her and also explained the story to a security guard at the station, who promised to keep a discreet eye on them when the man turned up. The DJ arrived on time and handed the girl back her bag, which still had everything in it except for her cash, and the girl thanked her Good Samaritan for his help. With that, he gave her his business card and left.

When the girl got home, she phoned the police to tell them her bag had been returned and was surprised when uniformed officers turned up on her doorstep within minutes. They asked for a statement and a description of the man and then told her that they were investigating four other handbag thefts in which the bags had been returned in exactly the same fashion, each of the previous victims being raped in their homes on the very evening the bags were returned. The police were convinced the man was making copies of house keys to enable him to commit his crimes. After a quick check, they found the telephone numbers on the business card to be false and the website address non-existent. Officers placed the house under observation and arrested

Jigsaw Premonition

In the heart of Dartmoor, an elderly widow lived alone. Her husband had died years previously and now the old lady lived frugally in her isolated cottage, passing her time completing jigsaw puzzles. One particularly foggy afternoon she ran out of puzzles and found herself with nothing to do. Deciding to go to bed early with a book, she heard a knock at the door and a muffled thump on the mat. She peered down the hallway to find a parcel wrapped in brown paper and tied with string lying on her doormat. When she opened the package, she was confronted with a new jigsaw puzzle but without a box and with no guiding picture. Being an expert, she went ahead anyway but was alarmed to find, as the picture developed in front of her, the scene was of her own front parlour, complete with the table she was sitting at and her chair, in which was an image of the old woman herself. As the last few pieces slotted into place, she noticed the window behind her seat had the image of a crazed-looking man holding an axe above his head and glaring in towards her. Nobody else heard the sound of breaking glass and the old woman's body lay undiscovered for three years. And police never found the prisoner who had escaped from Dartmoor Prison a few days before the old woman's demise . . .

The Legendary Hitch Hiker

And now for one of the most famous and oft-repeated legends of them all, about the missing hitch hiker. A man was driving home along an isolated country lane, miles from anywhere. As he rounded a sharp bend in the road, he saw, in his headlights, an attractive young girl standing alone, attempting to attract his attention. Drawing nearer, he noticed the girl was wearing evening dress and had obviously been to a party. Naturally he stopped and the girl got into the back of the car. He asked her how she had come to be in such an isolated place on her own so late at night, but the girl told him it was too long a story and she just wanted to get home. Assuming she had been abandoned by a heartless boyfriend, the driver asked for her address and set off to take her home. No conversation took place during the journey but when the man arrived at the address she had given him, he turned around to find the girl had vanished. The man was stunned, especially as he had not stopped the car at all, and there was no way the girl could have jumped out without him noticing. Still in shock, he walked up the pathway to the rambling house and rang the bell. An old man answered and listened as the driver told him the story of the hitch hiker. The old gentleman described the girl in perfect detail to the driver and then told him, 'She was my daughter, Luan. She died in a car accident on that bend some years ago and has been trying to get home ever since. So far she has not been able to make it.'

Other versions of this story that have appeared over the years include one of a man on a motorbike who picks up the girl only to find she has later vanished. He rides up and down the lane all night but can find no evidence at all that she had fallen off. There is also a version in which the driver lends the shivering girl his overcoat and drops her safely home. The following morning he realizes his coat is missing so calls round at the house only to be told the story of the girl's death. Refusing to believe her father, he is taken across the road to the cemetery and there, draped over her gravestone, is his overcoat.

The Missing Drivers

Legend has it that, in the deep and remote middle of America, engineers made a startling discovery while working on a road-widening project during the 1990s. Apparently one of the builders, during a lunch break, was kicking rocks off the side of the road and down into a deep canyon below when the sound of metal was heard. The foreman sent a man abseiling down the cliff face and there, perched on a ledge, was a 1950s Ford two-door sedan with the bodies of two women inside. A harness was attached and the car was winched back up to the road, police later revealing the two women had been reported missing after leaving a party in 1957, and nobody had seen or heard of them since.

It is a story with a common theme, and variations include a hunter in Norway, during the eighteenth century, who hit a church bell with one of his arrows deep in the northern wilderness. On further investigation, he discovered a lost village which had last been recorded during the Middle Ages and whose inhabitants had been wiped out by the Black Death. History, it would appear, had forgotten all about them.

It is not known whether or not either of these examples is true, but there have been news reports in America of the bodies of two girls found in a car submerged in a deep lake by bridge builders thirty-two years after they had been reported missing. In a similar vein, a fisherman in Norfolk was reported to have discovered a van submerged in a remote part of a canal, containing the bodies of five friends who had disappeared eighteen years earlier.

Buried Alive

The idea of being buried alive is just about everybody's worst nightmare. But while such stories are usually dismissed as pure fiction and simple scaremongering, the reality is that before the days of modern medicine, particularly before comas were fully understood, many people were interred, believed to be dead, when in fact they were still alive. There have been hundreds of exhumations in which the coffin lid was found to be scratched and the fingers of the body worn to the bone as the person had tried to dig himself out of his grave. While most cases naturally remain undetected, there are famous stories, some true, some perhaps no more than legends, confirming such misfortune. During the late seventeenth century – when, if your breath did not steam up a mirror, you were regarded as officially deceased – Matthew Wall had been pronounced dead and was being taken to his grave in the village of Braughing in Hertfordshire when one of his pallbearers slipped and dropped the coffin. This revived the 'deceased' and Wall went on to live many more years, each year famously celebrating his resurrection. He eventually died for real in 1695.

In one of the more famous cases, Anne Greene was hanged for felony on 14 December 1650 and taken to a medical laboratory for dissection.

Before the first incision was made, she fortunately revived and lived on for many more years. The murderer William Duell was hanged at Tyburn in November 1740, but prior to his dissection a laboratory assistant noticed a faint pulse. Within two hours, the executed man was sitting up and drinking wine. He was later transported for life. At around the same time, Professor Junker of Halle University in Germany had delivered to him a sack containing the body of a hanged man for dissection. But Junker had already retired for the night and the sack was dumped by his front door. During the night Junker was woken by someone tapping on his door, which he opened to reveal the 'dead' man, naked and freezing, holding the empty sack in his hands. After hearing the man's story, the good professor decided to help him escape further punishment and was delighted to meet him in the street, many years later, by then a prosperous and happily married merchant with two young children.

Marjorie Elphinstone 'died' during the early seventeenth century and was buried at Ardtannies in Scotland. Shortly after her funeral, grave robbers broke into the coffin, planning to steal her jewellery, but as they opened the coffin lid they found the terrified Marjorie alive and well. I doubt she was as terrified as they were when they fled the scene, and I imagine the men were probably haunted by the image for the rest of their lives. Marjorie, however, walked home and lived the rest of hers quite happily, including giving birth to two sons. In the end she outlived her husband by more than six years.

During the nineteenth century, William Tebb, a British merchant and critic of vaccination, recorded no fewer than 149 cases of premature burial, 219 cases of narrow escape from premature burial and ten cases of a dissection starting on a person who was not dead at the time. There are heartbreaking stories including the one of a young girl from South Carolina who 'died' of diphtheria while on holiday and was quickly interred in a local family's mausoleum for fear the disease might spread through the community. Many years later, when the mausoleum was next opened to admit the body of one of the family's own sons who had been killed during the Civil War, the tiny skeleton of the youngster was found behind the door. The terror of her final days does not bear thinking about.

In Naples, a lady was buried with all the expected formalities after being pronounced dead. Only a few weeks later, her grave was re-opened to receive another family member whose unfortunate predecessor was found with her clothing in tatters and several broken limbs, presumably caused by her trying to escape from the tomb. It was judged she had not been dead initially but simply in a trance. The doctor who had signed the death certificate and the mayor who had authorized the funeral were both later sentenced to three months in prison for involuntary manslaughter.

As recently as 1896, Mr T. M. Montgomery supervised the relocation of remains at the Fort Randall cemetery and recorded that 2 per cent of all those exhumed had shown signs of premature burial. Because of the advances in medical science, it is of course a situation far less common in modern times, but as recently as 1994 an 84-year-old lady, a Mildred C. Clarke, was found lying on her living room floor with no detectable heartbeat or pulse. She was pronounced dead at the scene and then spent ninety minutes in a body bag at the morgue before an assistant noticed the body was gently breathing beneath the bag. Mildred lived on for another week, after which it is to be hoped more thorough tests were carried out before she was taken to the morgue for a second time.

Don't Judge by Appearances

A young lady visiting Cape Town for the first time during the 1970s had been using the public transport system quite successfully, but remained mindful of the warning her local friends had given to her not to use the third-class carriage when travelling by train at night. However, one evening she had been forced to take the third-class carriage for a journey back to the city from Simon's Town and, with some reluctance, made her way to a seat. Glancing around the carriage, she noticed three young men on one side and a much older, wild-eyed, black man on the other. As she made her way to the seat, the black man stared at her and, when she chose a seat in front of the three youngsters for safety, he slowly shook his head at her. She noticed the two young men either side of their friend seemed to be holding him up, so she assumed he was drunk, but the wild-eyed man moved across the carriage and sat near her, holding his newspaper. She looked anxiously towards the younger men for support, but they ignored her attempts to catch their eye. The older man then gradually slid nearer, inching his way closer and closer to the young woman, who was, by then, approaching a state of panic. Eventually he leaned over and in a low, gruff voice said, 'Have you seen the news today, ma'am?' He held his newspaper up and, too terrified to move, she took a look at it. There, handwritten in ink, was a message from the man. It read: 'I'm a policeman, the man in the middle is dead and the other two have killed him. Get off at the next stop.'

HISTORICALLY SPEAKING

The Tsunami Bomb

The devastation caused in Southeast Asia by the cataclysmic tsunami wave on Boxing Day 2004 was a salutary reminder of the terrifying power of nature. Over 310,000 people lost their lives in many different countries, some as far distant as five thousand miles from the earthquake that triggered the catastrophe. Nobody could fail to be moved by the images beamed around the world of entire regions simply erased by the giant wave in one of the worst natural disasters in history. But, for some onlookers, the events also served as a reminder of something that, until recently, had been regarded as no more than a dark rumour – the Tsunami Bomb.

Professor Thomas Leech, an Australian, was awarded a CBE in 1947 for his work on developing a secret weapon, given the name Project Seal. No further details were released at the time, as work was 'ongoing and top secret', although many stories arose, fuelled by speculation. However, declassification of some top-secret military files in the year 2000 revealed the deadly nature of the professor's work. (Leech was no longer alive at this point, having died back in 1973.)

In 1915, during the early years of the First World War, a ship packed with weapons exploded in the English Channel causing a mini tidal wave. Those witnessing the effects recalled the eruption of Krakatoa in 1883 that triggered a tidal wave resulting in 36,000 deaths in the area. The accident in 1915 gave rise to the idea of deliberately generating such a phenomenon by using underwater explosives, and so Project Seal was established.

In 1944 and 1945 Leech, who had been seconded to the army, created a series of explosions in the sea off Whangaparaoa in New Zealand. Waves thirty feet high were generated by the explosions, and the tests were considered to be so significant and successful that a member of the US Board of Assessors of Atomic Tests, Dr Karl Compton, was dispatched to New Zealand to consider the results. A letter from the US government to the New Zealand authorities in Wellington followed the visit, stating: 'Dr Compton is impressed with Professor Leech's deductions on the Seal Project and is prepared to recommend to the Joint Chiefs of Staff that all technical data from the test relevant to the Seal Project should be made available to the New Zealand government for further study by

Professor Leech.' In addition, US authorities considered sending Professor Leech to Bikini Atoll to witness the nuclear tests there in the hope they might assist Project Seal.

It would appear, too, that the US and British governments were seriously considering Project Seal as a realistic alternative to dropping the atom bomb on Japan in 1945, with the added benefit of it appearing to the world as a natural disaster. Defence chiefs are known to have believed that if the Tsunami Bomb had been fully developed by the end of the war, it would undoubtedly have been used and a manmade wave could have flattened Japan.

In addition to this, after the fall of the Soviet Union in 1991, evidence suggested that Russian scientists had been extensively researching Tsunami Bomb technology during the Cold War with a view to destroying large areas of southern England and Holland while avoiding the problems of radiation fall-out created by a nuclear attack. Which is very considerate of them, isn't it?

Robin Hood

The tale of Robin Hood is one of the great English legends. For generations we have been told about this lovable bandit who famously stole from the rich and gave to the poor and who

lived with Maid Marian and his Merry Men in Sherwood Forest, near Nottingham. Over the years, he has been the subject of songs and ballads, radio and TV programmes, novels, films, paintings and poems. He has been portrayed as farmer, archer, nobleman, hero, traitor and common thief, but what do we really know about him? Most of the information about Robin Hood has been gleaned from the ballads and tales that have been passed down from generation to generation, the best known including 'Robin Hood and the Curtal Friar' (in which he meets Friar Tuck), 'Robin Hood and Guy of Gisborne' and 'Robin Hood's Death', all of which were written down before 1550, while variations upon them have been retold ever since. Although some of the ballads make reference to the Sheriff of

Nottingham, Robin Hood's band of Merry Men and other figures involved with the outlaw, there is no mention at all of Maid Marian, so it would appear she has been added in as Robin's love interest in later tales.

The earliest written reference to Robin appeared as early as 1377, in the poem *Piers Plowman*, which includes the lines:

I do not know my paternoster perfectly as the priest
    sings it,
But I know rhymes of Robin Hood and Randolph,
    Earl of Chester . . .
(I kan noght parfitly my Paternoster as the preest it
    syngeth,
But I kan rymes of Robyn Hood and Randolf Erl of
    Chestre . . .)

Although Robin Hood truly has earned the status of a legend through these ballads and poems, there is evidence to suggest that he may have actually been a real historical figure. One claim is that he lived between 1160 and 1247 and is buried at Kirklees Priory in West Yorkshire. It is said that Robin (or Robert) had been made Earl of Huntingdon by Richard the Lionheart during the Crusades before being killed by Sir Roger of Doncaster and his own cousin, the Prioress of Kirklees, when he travelled to visit them at the priory – which would account for why he is buried there. The Kirklees Priory now lies in ruins, but a medieval tombstone, which can be seen to this day, would seem to support this theory:

> Hear undernead dis laitl stean
> Lais Robert Earl of Huntingtun
> Near arcir der as hie sa geud
> An pipl kauld im Robin Heud
> Sic utlaws as hi an is men
> Vil England nivr si agen.

> Obiit 24 Kal Dekembris 1247

Then there is the hollow tree in Sherwood Forest he supposedly lived in, the Major Oak. Some historians have dismissed Robin Hood as purely mythical partly on the basis that the Major Oak is not old enough to have existed in the thirteenth century, when Robin was supposed to have inhabited Sherwood Forest. In fact the famous tree has been carbon dated at between 800 and 1,000 years of age, meaning it could even have been as much as 250 years old at the time Robin was alive, making it an ancient tree even then. Other disputed facts centre on Robin's birthplace being Lockersley, which, as is sometimes pointed out, does not exist. But if the town of Robin's birth is Loxley, that certainly does exist, a small village close to Stratford-upon-Avon, overlooking the Avon Valley. A church has stood there since the eighth century, the tower of the present church dating back to the 1100s, while in the churchyard a gravestone from the thirteenth century bears the name Robert Fitz Odo, which some people believe to have been the name given to Robin of Loxley at birth.

So could there have been two Robin Hoods? That would certainly explain some of the discrepancies in the stories about him. As it was another two centuries before Caxton invented his printing press, most information would have been passed around by word of mouth, so it is easy to see how two similar figures could morph into one in the stories. Just imagine: two national heroes battling on the side of the poor and raging against injustice and the decadence of the rich. If they had known about each other, they could have started a revolution, or a trade union. They would have kept Maid Marian busy too.

Hotel Mystery

A story has been told around Europe since the 1890s of a young English woman who rushed into the British Embassy in Paris, at the time of the great exhibition of 1889, in a state of great distress. After being comforted, she told officials that she and her mother had taken two single rooms in a Parisian hotel and that her mother had booked into Room 223. She had soon become concerned for her mother, however, who had collapsed on the bed complaining of stomach pains.

A doctor was immediately sent for and, having examined the old lady in private, he explained that she was seriously ill and that her daughter should take his carriage to carry a note to his wife at the surgery and return with the necessary drugs. He told her it was only a short distance away, but the driver appeared to take a long route, as it was a full two hours before the young woman reached the doctor's surgery. She finally arrived back at the hotel with the medicine to be met with blank stares from the reception staff. The manager she had spoken to only four hours earlier also looked blankly at her, before saying, 'Madame, you must have made a mistake. You arrived here alone and we know nothing about your mother.' The doctor seemed similarly confused and confirmed he too knew nothing of her mother. The girl demanded to be taken to Room 223 and she found it empty, although the furnishings appeared to have changed. The velvet curtains, formerly a deep blue, were now green and the wallpaper was plain instead of floral-patterned. The only luggage to be found was not her mother's and appeared to belong to strangers. The young lady then demanded to see the guest book and again no trace of her mother's name was evident. The hotel staff merely shrugged at her continued entreaties, and it was at this point that the girl fled to the British Embassy. Here she was treated with compassion but her story regarded with disbelief, although staff remained suspicious that the hotel and doctor were colluding to cover up the old lady's death in an attempt to avoid bad publicity. In the absence of any firm evidence, however, the young lady was returned to England and, despite her protests, confined to a mental institution for the rest of her life.

This unfortunate sequence of events reminds us of a famous *Fawlty Towers* episode where hotel boss Basil and his staff go to extraordinary lengths to conceal the body of a dead man from other guests in the hotel. To escape from the mayhem he has created, Basil finally jumps into a laundry basket, formerly used to hide the dead body, and is carried out to the waiting laundry lorry and driven away.

The One-man World War

Hiroo Onoda was working for the Tajima Yoko trading company in Hanokow, China, when the Second World War broke out, and in August 1942, aged twenty, he returned home to Waka-yama in Japan where he joined the Japanese army. He trained as an officer at the Imperial Army Intelligence School, receiving instruction in guerrilla warfare, survival techniques and

intelligence gathering, before being sent to the
Philippines. There he was ordered to lead the
Lubang garrison in a campaign of guerrilla warfare, and as he prepared to join the action, his
division commander, Major Taniguchi, gave him
his final orders: 'You are completely forbidden
to die by your own hand. It may take three
years, it may take six, but whatever happens
we will come back for you. Until we do and as
long as you have one soldier to command, you
must continue to lead him. You may have to
live on only coconuts and, if so, that is what
you must do. Under no circumstances must you
give up your life voluntarily.' With those words
resonating in his head, he left, on 17 December
1944, for Lubang Island, located between the
Philippine Sea and the South China Sea, with
orders to destroy the airfield, lay explosives at the
pier and generally sabotage the Allied campaign.

However, soon the Allied forces had overrun
the island and, after brief resistance, during
which Onoda lost many of his men, his unit
was forced to retreat to the inner and remote
areas of Lubang in order to regroup. After several
attacks and the loss of many more soldiers,
Onoda decided to split the remaining men into
cells of four. His group included Corporal
Shoichi Shimada, aged thirty, Private Yuichi
Akatsu, aged twenty-two, and the 24-year-old
Private Kinshichi Kozuka. The four lived in self-
made shelters with limited ammunition, very few

supplies, just the clothes they were wearing and a rifle each. Between them they survived on coconuts, bananas, fresh rainwater and any animal they could catch and kill, including the odd cow. After virtually all of the groups of men were either captured or killed over the following year, Onoda decided his cell should remain hidden and be used only for guerrilla raids on known Allied positions. Then in October 1945, when Onoda was visiting a farm in search of a cow, he found a leaflet, which read: 'The war ended on 15 August. Come down from the mountains.' The leaflet did not make sense to Onoda as his cell had been fired upon only weeks earlier, so the four men decided it must have been left by enemy soldiers attempting to coax them out into the open. They didn't fall for it and remained hidden.

Many times over the next few years, islanders tried to contact Onoda and even flew an aircraft over the mountain region, dropping leaflets reproducing the Japanese surrender order signed by General Yamashita, but the men believed this also to be a hoax. The islanders repeatedly called out over loudspeakers in areas all over the mountains, but Onoda and his men responded only by firing on them. Presumably the letters and photographs from friends and relatives at home in Japan were not enough to persuade Onoda and his men either. It appeared that nothing could make them believe the war was really over.

Year after year, the four men eked out their existence and fired at villagers or holidaymakers who stumbled upon the group, believing them to be enemy soldiers in disguise. Then, in September 1949, the resolve of Private Yuichi Akatsu finally broke and he managed to walk away from the others and survive alone for six further months in the jungle before eventually surrendering. The other three – who presumably had found wild cannabis plants growing in the region, given the state of their paranoia – regarded this as a security leak and, sure enough, when Akatsu later returned with news that the war really was over, they shot at him. In June 1953, a full eight years after the war had formally ended and everyone else had gone home, Corporal Shoichi Shimada was wounded in a skirmish with a search party. Despite the group having no medicine or first aid equipment, his leg injury slowly healed, although he finally died nearly a year later in May 1954 after attacking local fishermen. They returned fire and killed him on the beach, leaving just two men. And this is how it stayed over the next eighteen years with both men hiding out on the remote island waiting for their next orders from the Imperial Army, all the time reminding themselves of their divisional commander's final words: 'Whatever happens, we will come back for you.'

The two men were officially declared dead in December 1959, but in October 1972, at the age of fifty-one, Private Kinshichi Kozuka was killed by a Philippine army patrol. The episode led to speculation that Onoda might also still be alive, and efforts were renewed to find him and put an end to the one-man world war he was waging. Search parties were dispatched but Onoda managed to remain hidden. That was until a Japanese student called Norio Suzuki announced to his friends he was going to travel the world to find 'a panda, the abominable snowman and Lieutenant Hiroo Onoda', and where so many others had failed, he actually succeeded. At first he tried to convince Onoda the war had been over for many years, but failed to persuade the ageing soldier. However, Onoda had become weary of being alone and made one concession: he would return home on the condition that his former commanding officer ordered him to. Suzuki travelled back to Japan and discovered that luckily Major Taniguchi was still alive. The former officer agreed to return to Lubang Island, and on 9 March 1974 Major Taniguchi formally ordered Onoda to cease all combat duties with immediate effect, and the weary mountain soldier came down from the hills. For a little while the news that the war was over failed to sink in properly, but when it did, Onoda's response was: 'We really lost the war? How could they have been so stupid!' Presumably the irony of those words being uttered by a man who had spent nearly thirty years living under a rock, for no reason at all, was lost on Onoda, but there was worse to come and the man himself describes the moment in his autobiography:

Suddenly everything went black and a storm raged inside me. I felt like a fool for having been so tense and cautious on the way down here. Worse than that, what had I been doing for all of these years? But gradually the storm subsided and for the first time I really understood my thirty years of guerrilla warfare were over. It was the end. I pulled back my rifle bolt and emptied it of shells. I eased off the pack I always carried with me and laid the gun on top of it. Would I really have no more use for the rifle I had polished and cared for like a baby all these years? Or Kozuka's rifle, which I had hidden in a crevice in the rocks? Had the war really ended thirty years ago? If it had, what had Shimada and Kozuka died for? If what was happening was really true then wouldn't it have been better if I had died with them?

During their many years on the island, Onoda and his men had killed at least thirty Filipinos and had wounded over a hundred more. But after formally surrendering to the Philippine president, Ferdinand Marcos, Onoda was officially pardoned and allowed to return to Japan as a national hero, receiving world media attention on his arrival back home. Finding life in Japan to be very different from what he had known all those years before, he moved to a remote farm in Brazil where he wrote his memoirs, entitled *No Surrender: My Thirty-Year War*, published in December 1974. He travelled back to Lubang Island in 1996 to lay a wreath at the war memorial before marrying a Japanese lady and returning to his homeland to fund a nature reserve camp for children. Remarkably, at the time of writing this in 2006, Hiroo Onoda is still alive and at eighty-five years old lives quietly with his wife in Japan. The story in circulation before 1974 about the lone Japanese soldier living in a jungle, refusing to believe the war was over, was no myth or urban legend after all – it was a true one.

The Olympic Marathon Legend

The word 'marathon' and its association with the longest Olympic event all began with the legend of Pheidippides, a Greek soldier who apparently ran from the town of Marathon to Athens in 460 BC, bearing the news that the Persian army had been defeated at the Battle of Marathon. Pheidippides, we are told, died of exhaustion as soon as he had delivered the words: 'Rejoice, we conquer.' There is no actual evidence of the soldier's great feat, but the first account of a run from Marathon to Athens appears in Plutarch's *On the Glory of Athens*, written during the first century AD. It is generally assumed that the distance of today's modern Olympic marathon must be carefully measured to match, to the exact inch, the distance Pheidippides covered on that eventful day, but the International Olympic Committee has estimated the distance from the Marathon battlefield to Athens to be 21.4 miles and not the 26 miles 385 yards athletes cover in modern events. To find out where the extra mileage came from, we need to know more about the event itself and how it has developed over the years.

The initial competitive marathon was held as the final event in the 1896 Olympic Games in Athens, said to mark the revival of the race, but there is no record of one taking place before then. During the planning of the Athens Games, the French historian Michel Bréal suggested the event – a race set at 24.8 miles – in order to commemorate Pheidippides' run. The importance of the event was raised to new levels when the Greek people, disappointed at daily defeats by American and European athletes, began to offer rewards to the eventual winner of the marathon, as long as he was Greek. Georgios Averoff, one of the financiers of the new Olympic stadium, offered his daughter's hand in marriage along with a dowry of a million drachmas (£1.2 million, in today's money), while other locals joined in the fun by offering free haircuts for life, free wine, cattle, jewellery, clothing and even free supplies of food for life, so long as the winner was Greek.

The odds were good as, at the starting line, twenty-one out of twenty-five of the runners were Greek, the remaining four coming from France, America, Hungary and Australia. As the race drew to a close, three of the four non-Greeks held the first three places, but as they neared the stadium, first the American, then the Frenchman and finally the Australian all collapsed from exhaustion, leaving a little-known Greek runner, Spiridon 'Spiros' Louis, to sneak into first place with a seven-minute lead. His final approach, to the stadium, had been crowded with Greek fans urging on their countryman. Prince George and Prince Constantine had run the final few laps inside the stadium with Spiridon, before hoisting him on to their shoulders and carrying him to their father, King George, in his royal box. Crowds both inside the stadium and thronging the surrounding hills cheered with joy and women threw their jewellery at his feet. Greece had a new hero.

Spiridon became a wealthy man but little is known of his later years. One thing is certain, he did not accept Averoff's daughter as his wife because he was already married at the time. For the record, 'Spiros' won the race in 2 hours 58 minutes and 50 seconds, including stopping along the way for a glass of wine with his uncle, who was waiting for him at the village of Chalandri.

The distance the athletes covered varied over the following thirty years; then in 1908, during the London Olympics, the royal family asked for the race to start at Windsor Castle so that their children could watch it. The distance from Windsor Castle to the Olympic Stadium in White City, London, where the track and field events were held, is exactly 26 miles 385 yards, and this has become the standard length for all marathons staged since 1924. So the distance of the modern marathon wasn't set by the great run itself, following the Battle of Marathon in 460 BC, but was determined by the British royal family, to keep their children happy, in 1908 – which dispels another legend once and for all.

Spare Ribs

For many years, rumour has circulated about a particular celebrity who, in search of the perfect waistline, has actually had ribs removed so that she can appear slimmer and squeeze herself into even tinier outfits. This would be the modern-day equivalent of the whalebone corset our fashionable female forbears used to squeeze into, so that men could encircle their wasp-sized waists with both hands. The story has been told over the years about actresses such as Elizabeth Taylor, Jane Fonda, Pamela Anderson, Gina Lollobrigida and Raquel Welch. Singers, although I use the term loosely, like Janet Jackson and Britney Spears, are also said to have taken such steps, along with the models Kate Moss and Stephanie Seymour. Even the male singer Marilyn Manson is said to have succumbed to vanity in this way.

This urban legend harks back to the Victorian era when trendy London socialites are believed to have had their lowest pair of ribs removed to provide fashionable waistlines, but although it is possible one or two wealthy women discussed this as an option, there is no medical evidence of it ever being carried out. It is also as well to remember that during the nineteenth century cosmetic surgery was unheard of and surgery of any kind was regarded as extremely dangerous. Surgical hygiene was only in its infancy, methods of sedation were crude and unsafe, and the chances of survival were far lower than they are today. The effect of germs was still not properly understood, despite the pioneering work being conducted by Louis Pasteur in the latter half of the century, and penicillin had yet to be discovered. The fatality rate from amputations was high and there is no reason to believe the unnecessary removal of perfectly good ribs would have enjoyed a greater success rate. Such considerations and the fact that no evidence of rib removal can be found indicate that this legend, certainly when applied to the nineteenth century, must be untrue. In modern times, while ribs can be removed with relative impunity, it seems highly improbable that anyone has ever requested it.

In a similar vein is the notion that certain actresses or models would go as far as having their wisdom teeth removed to make their faces appear slimmer and to accentuate their cheekbones, and, again, nobody has ever gone on record to state this as the reason for having their wisdom teeth removed. So while this may be more plausible than rib removal, it is also, I suspect, only a myth.

The Madness of King George

For the last decade, the story has been told that the hit British film *The Madness of King George*, released in 1994, had its title changed from *The Madness of George III* for American audiences in the belief the US public would be stupid enough to think the film was a sequel and they had missed parts one and two. According to the story, the film might be regarded as the final part of a trilogy and so people would not go and see it until they had viewed the first two, which, of course, did not exist, and this is why the 'III' was dropped from the title.

The film documented the behaviour of British

monarch King George III, who periodically lost his marbles after losing the North American colonies during the American Revolution in the 1780s. His condition is now believed to have been due to a rare hereditary disorder called porphyria that, as the king found, is both physically and mentally debilitating. It was a fascinating film, starring Nigel Hawthorne and Helen Mirren, but the myth about the title should never have arisen. For a start, the English version of the film was never called *The Madness of George III*. There is indeed a very successful play of that name by Alan Bennett, on which the film is based, but it was decided very early on by the film producers to call the movie *The Madness of King George* as they felt it important to have the word 'king' in the title, for the benefit of a worldwide audience unfamiliar with British history – and that is the sole reason for the change.

There have been other examples of titles being changed to help the overseas viewer understand the subject of the film. For example, the film about the relationship between Queen Victoria and her Scottish servant John Brown, played by Judi Dench and Billy Connolly, was entitled *Mrs Brown* in Britain, where audiences understood the connection, but *Her Majesty, Mrs Brown* for overseas release.

The Legend of Dick Turpin

Richard Turpin was born in the Old Post Cottage on 21 September 1705 in the tranquil village of Hempstead, hidden away in rural Essex. His grandfather had been a farmer but Richard's father became the keeper of The Bell Inn that still stands today and is now called The Rose and Crown. For many years, the tavern was frequented by smugglers, becoming a hive of criminal activity, and it is likely Turpin was introduced to a life of crime at an early age. At sixteen years old, the future highwayman moved to the village of Whitechapel on the outskirts of London and became an apprentice butcher. Although described as 'loose, disorderly and lazy', he completed his apprenticeship and managed to open his own butcher's shop in Buckhurst Hill, Essex, after marrying his childhood sweetheart, Elizabeth Millington, in 1728.

This was when Turpin began his criminal activities in earnest, by stocking his butcher's shop window not with legitimate cuts of farmed meat, but with cattle, sheep and lamb he had stolen from local farmers. In short, he had become a rustler – in the early 1700s an offence punishable by death. His business prospered, however, and he became well known locally, until one day he attempted to steal a pair of oxen and was caught red-handed. Worse than that, the farmer recognized the butcher and Turpin was forced to abandon his wife and business and flee the area. For a few years, he lay low in the Essex wilderness where he survived by robbing smugglers also hiding out in the area. Soon he moved to Epping Forest where, in 1735, he met the notorious Essex Gang, also known as the Gregory Gang. A band of twenty thieves, they lived in caves in the forest and modelled themselves on the legend of Robin Hood. But they were a ruthless bunch who preyed on rural farmers and passing nobility. They stole and ate royal game, an offence punishable by hanging, drawing and quartering, and they raped and pillaged for miles around, the *London Evening Post* reporting their misdemeanours on a regular basis. As a result, they soon grew notorious throughout the land and the king offered a substantial reward for their capture.

The gang were soon betrayed and were cornered in a tavern in Westminster, but Turpin managed to escape by jumping from a window. Three ringleaders were caught and hanged and the rest dispersed, too scared to meet again – the Gregory Gang was disbanded. However, Turpin returned to Epping Forest and became the famous highwayman he is remembered as, attacking hundreds of stagecoaches as they travelled through the forest. As London was essentially a lawless place in those days, the wealthy would often travel with their valuables and Turpin realized this made them an easy target in the isolated forest. Within a year he had retired to Yorkshire, but this was not when he made his fabled fifteen-hour ride on Black Bess from London to York and subsequent safety. Sadly, Turpin never did – that part of his legend is simply made up. Instead, he changed his name to John Palmer and travelled at leisure as a wealthy man. But old habits die hard, and in Yorkshire John Palmer was arrested for sheep stealing and poaching game birds. No one suspected he was actually the famous fugitive highwayman until, while trapped inside York prison, he wrote to his brother-in-law, back in his hometown of Hempstead, asking for an alibi. This is when Turpin's luck ran out as his brother-in-law, unaware of who John Palmer was and failing to recognize the handwriting, refused to pay the required postage fee. But a local schoolmaster caught a glimpse of the letter as it was being returned and recognized his old pupil's hand. He reported this to the authorities and subsequently claimed the £200 reward on Turpin's head, a considerable sum of money in the mid 1700s.

Turpin was immediately tried for a long list of offences, found guilty and sentenced to be hanged. It was only then that he became the celebrity he was supposed to have been in life and received many visitors before his execution.

On 7 April 1739, Turpin secured his legendary status by cheating the hangman of his duty and launching himself into eternity by jumping off the scaffold, dying within five minutes. And so the Dick Turpin legend was born, although in reality he was not the gallant highwayman we believed him to be, but a simple rustler turned armed robber.

Captain Kidd the Pirate

As any schoolboy will confirm, Captain Kidd is the most famous pirate of all time. Unfortunately, Captain Kidd was not strictly speaking a pirate. At forty years old, William Kidd was a respected English sea captain with a first-class record. His reliability was the reason the British government invited him to lead a privateering expedition in 1695. In centuries past, ships that displayed the flags of nations England was at war with were regarded as fair game and a privateer was permitted to attack and loot the cargo of any enemy merchant vessels. As Kidd sailed, he knew England was once again at war with France. Essentially these men were 'authorized pirates' and they were also given permission to confront *unlicensed* privateers (pirates) while at sea. In other words, with permission a ship's captain might steal the cargo of a ship registered with a nation England was at war with. Not having the correct authority on the other hand meant being a common pirate.

As Kidd's small fleet patrolled the Red Sea, he sighted two Armenian ships – sailing, as it turned out, under French passes – and duly intercepted them, as he was legally entitled to do. But the ships' owners complained to the authorities in London and, in what appears to be a case of politics in action, Kidd was amazed to find himself arrested when he later docked in New York, and branded a pirate. The captain protested his innocence and forwarded the French passes to the correct authorities in England, fully expecting to be exonerated when he returned to London. But during the two years before his case was submitted to the magistrate, the passes (Kidd's proof) disappeared and he was convicted and hanged on 23 May 1701. The best-known pirate of them all was, in fact, an innocent man, a victim of behind-the-scenes skulduggery and the Old Boys' Network.

The Great Fire of London

There are two popular myths concerning the Great Fire of London, which devastated the city in 1666, destroying 13,200 houses and 87 churches. The first is that the fire had been started deliberately in a bakehouse by a French Catholic and the second is that it brought about the end of the rat-carried bubonic plague responsible for 50,000 deaths during 1665, although many historians now believe as many as 500,000 lives could have been lost.

Europe was in religious turmoil during the mid seventeenth century, with war raging on all sides. The French, Spanish, Irish and Italians were all Catholic countries while England remained a firmly Protestant nation, although its monarch, Charles II, had strong links with Catholic France as he had lived there and in Holland since the execution of his father, Charles I, in 1649. In 1665, England looked as though it would lose the war with the Dutch and the English were in a state of high anxiety. Many even blamed the Plague on the Catholics and, when the city catastrophically burned the following year, natives were looking for a Catholic scapegoat. They found one in the shape of a simpleton watchmaker called Thomas Hubert, who also happened to be a French Catholic. Hubert confessed to starting the fire deliberately in Westminster and was promptly arrested. It was then pointed out the fire had not been started in Westminster and had not even reached there but had begun in Thomas Farriner's bakery in Pudding Lane, so Hubert changed his story and confessed to starting it there instead. Despite not being able to describe the bakery or even to explain where it was, he was hauled before the court. Three of the panel of judges were members of Farriner's own family, who strongly denied responsibility for the devastating fire, and although confirmation was given that Hubert had not even arrived in London until two days after the blaze had started, his confession was accepted and he was hanged on the gibbet at Tyburn.

Nobody knows why Hubert insisted on his responsibility, but in the seventeenth century the fact that he was both French and a Catholic, not to mention stupid, was enough to hang him. Catholic-baiting continued over the coming years and further smaller fires gave rise to similar accusations from Londoners. When the monument was finally erected to commemorate the Great Fire, it displayed an inscription reading: 'The burning of this Protestant City was begun and carried on by the treachery and malice of the Popish faction.' This was removed during the Catholic rule of James II between 1685 and 1689 but soon reappeared and stayed in place until the more tolerant nineteenth century, when it was finally removed for good in 1831. Contrary to popular opinion, the Great Fire did not kill thousands of Londoners. In fact, the fire spread so slowly, giving plenty of time for escape, that official records cite only five deaths – a baker's maid, who was too frightened to climb to safety over the roof with the rest of the family and was left behind, a shoemaker, an elderly gentleman who died trying to retrieve his blanket from

St Paul's Cathedral and two people who fell into their cellars while trying to protect their possessions by moving them underground.

It is also widely believed that the Great Fire was responsible for killing London's rats, the known carriers of the Plague, but this is also untrue, mainly because the fire was contained in the city of London and did not actually reach any parish affected by the disease, these parishes being to the north and west of the fire. The result would have been to drive more rats into those areas, not to reduce numbers overall.

As the winter of 1665 set in, the cold harsh weather severely restricted the reproductive activity of the *Ceratophyllus fasciatus* (rat flea) and the *Rattus Rattus* (black rat), the main carriers of the plague bacillus. This caused a temporary reduction in the rodent and flea population of London and a short relief from the effects of the Plague. But, more importantly, there had been increasing numbers of survivors after each outbreak, indicating a growing immunity among the population of London, and this, added to the fact that each outbreak resulted in decreasing virulence of the disease itself, is the main reason for it dying out in London. It is generally believed that the fatal strain would soon have been weakened to the point of no longer being fatal before disappearing altogether. But the fire will have had some effect in that replacing the squalid wooden structures destroyed by the blaze with brick buildings would have significantly reduced the number of rats and fleas in the area, driving them into less populated areas where infection was less likely to rise to the epidemic levels it had reached in the cramped, densely populated city of the time. Rapid improvements in medicine and hygiene killed off any remaining strains of the Plague and London has remained free from its grip ever since.

Stanford University

There is a story that has circled the globe for decades about the origins of Stanford University in California, and it goes something like this. A man in a homemade and well-worn suit and a lady in a threadbare, faded gingham dress walked into the office of the president of Harvard University and asked for a meeting with the president, without having made an appointment. The secretary assumed from the appearance of the couple that they were simple country folk, and did not want to waste the president's valuable time. She frowned at the couple and snapped, 'He is unavailable and will be busy all day.' The couple announced they would wait for as long as they had to and took seats in the outer office. For most of the morning, the secretary ignored them in the hope they would leave, but finally she went in to the president and explained the situation to him in the hope he could have a few quick words with them and they would then go home. Somewhat annoyed, he agreed for the couple to be shown into his office.

Once they'd been shown in, the president took one look at them and let out an exasperated sigh. The lady spoke first: 'We had a son who attended Harvard for a year but a few months ago he was killed in an accident. My husband and I would like to erect a memorial to him here at Harvard University.' The president was surprised but explained to the lady that they could not possibly build a statue for every former Harvard student who died as the place would 'look like a graveyard'. 'That isn't what we meant,' the lady replied. 'We want to donate a building to Harvard.' The president grew frustrated and snapped, 'A building? Do you have any idea at all how much a building would cost? We have over seven and a half million dollars' worth of buildings here!' The lady fell silent and the president hoped he'd put them off, with their ridiculous far-fetched ideas, and encouraged them to leave. Instead, the lady turned to her husband and said, 'Seven and a half million dollars to build a university – is that all it costs? Why don't we just build our own?' Her husband silently nodded and they got up and left. The president, somewhat bewildered by now, called the couple back to ask their names. 'I am Jane Stanford,' the lady replied, 'and this is my husband Leland Stanford, the railroad billionaire.' In 1891, the couple opened the doors to the now world-famous Stanford University at Palo Alto in California.

It is a fascinating story and would be even better were it true, but sadly it isn't. Despite being believed by millions across the globe, it is simply an urban legend. For a start, it is highly unlikely the president of Harvard University would not have recognized Leland Stanford, one of the most famous businessmen of his day in America, not to mention also being the elected governor of California at the time and a member of the US Senate. Even if he did fail to recognize him, it is unlikely Governor Stanford would not introduce himself properly in the first place. The true story of what happened can be found on the University of Stanford website, which even has a section dispelling what they call the 'gingham dress legend'.

In the true version of the story, the family was on holiday in Italy during 1884 when fifteen-year-old Leland junior contracted typhoid fever and on 13 March he died at the Hotel Bristol in Florence. Leland Stanford then announced to his wife, 'The children of California shall be our children,' and he vowed to invest in education in the memory of his son. On returning to America, the ship docked at New York and the couple took the opportunity to seek the advice of prominent education officials on the East Coast before they set off on the journey home to California. They did indeed visit President Eliot of Harvard University and discussed with him their ideas for the funding of a university, a technical school or a museum and lecture facility in their home town of Palo Alto. Eliot advised them a university would give the state's children the most benefit, and when Stanford asked him how much the proposal was likely to cost him, Eliot replied it would be 'no less than five million dollars'. There was then a long pause before Stanford turned to his wife and said, 'Well, Jane, I think we could manage that, couldn't we?' Jane Stanford nodded in agreement and Stanford University was conceived at that moment.

INTELLECTUALLY CHALLENGED

Unplugged

A hospital bed in the intensive care ward of a major hospital became notorious and feared throughout the campus. The reason was that, for the previous three months, every single patient to occupy that particular bed had died within a day of being moved there. The authorities suspected foul play and took the decision to set up 24-hour observation by fitting hidden CCTV cameras focusing on the bed in question. It wasn't long before the reason for the tragedies became apparent.

The following morning, one of the cleaning contractors entered the room with a mechanical floor polisher, unplugged the patient's life-support machine, plugged in the polisher and spent ten minutes cleaning the floor. She then replaced the plug and moved on to the next room, unaware that she had left the patient lying dead.

Dough for Brains

It was a hot summer's day in Middle America when a young man pulled into a parking space outside his local superstore. As he got out of the car, he noticed a lady in the bay next to him slumped over the steering wheel of her car, holding the back of her head. Believing her to be asleep, he went off to go about his business and only began to grow concerned when, on returning an hour or so later, he found the lady in exactly the same position. This time he was worried and rapped on the driver's window, asking if she needed any help. The woman didn't move but called out, 'Please dial 911, as I have been shot and I can feel my brains seeping out.' On closer inspection, the man noticed a grey, sticky substance oozing between her fingers and so he sprinted back into the shopping complex to call for help. An ambulance raced to the scene and paramedics quickly examined the injured lady, also inspecting her hand. On checking the rest of the car, they all started to laugh. Onlookers were appalled until paramedics explained the victim had a canister of fresh biscuit dough on top of one of the shopping bags on the back seat. The intense heat had caused the tube to explode with the metal lid hitting the lady on the back of the head, shooting out grey dough, which had then stuck to her hair. Once she had been helped from the car, the lady sheep-ishly explained she had sat there, afraid to move and waiting for help, for over two hours. The shop manager offered a free packet of dough in compensation. Good Ol' America, I say.

Rookie Robberies

There is nothing quite as rewarding as reading a supposedly true story of a would-be armed criminal who is so spectacularly inept we can only laugh. In a world-class example of how not to rob a post office, a 32-year-old Manchester man began by forgetting to wear his mask, which meant his crime was recorded on CCTV cameras. Secondly he was unaware the safe was held shut by a timed locking system, which he had missed by ten minutes, so he had to make do with the small change from the tills, which was handed to him in cash bags. Because the bags were so heavy, he enlisted the help of two local youths, who not only held the doors open for him but also helped to carry the bags to his car. As it was rush hour, the two lads were able to walk behind the car for about a mile, noting the registration number before the thief waved goodbye as the traffic cleared. When he later arrived at a motorway hotel, he asked staff to place the cash bags in the safe before asking them not to tell the police where he was. After his arrest, a short while later, the chap denied all allegations, although when asked for his occupation, replied, 'Armed Robber.'

It's hard to believe anyone could be quite so feather-brained, until you read the story of another would-be armed robber and his ill-conceived bid to join the criminal underworld. Police later found no history of crime on his personal records but, from the circumstances of his initial attempt, that could be easily explained. First of all was his choice of target, the R&J Firearms Warehouse in Ohio, a state where it is perfectly legal for adults to carry guns. Then there was the small fact of a police patrol car being parked outside the entrance and the police officer standing at the counter having coffee with the warehouse owner.

Quite what possessed the chap then to announce a hold-up and fire two shots into the air is anybody's guess, but both the police officer and the warehouse owner immediately returned fire, killing him instantly. According to police reports and witness statements, as many as twenty-five customers also drew their guns but no other shots were fired and nobody else was hurt in the incident.

Winnebago Whiner

The contender for Idiot of the Year staked her claim after buying a brand new 32-foot Winnebago from a dealership in her hometown of Darwin, Australia. On her first long journey, as soon as she reached the main highway she, remarkably, set the vehicle on to cruise control, left the driver's seat and went into the back to make some coffee. It is quite extraordinary that she was not injured at all when the RV left the road and overturned before coming to a standstill sixty yards deep in the bush. Apparently not the least embarrassed by her actions, the woman then tried to sue Winnebago for not making it clear in the owner's manual that cruise control as she understood it was not a feature of the vehicle. The result of any lawsuit, if in fact one took place at all, is not recorded, which leads us to believe this story is simply an urban legend. It has to be, doesn't it? Nobody can be that stupid and still be able to afford a motor home like that.

More Prize Idiots

The following is a selection of my favourite, apparently true examples of complete foolishness, bordering on the brainless. It makes us wonder how these people survive in life, but far from dismissing those involved, who will for obvious reasons remain nameless, we should be grateful for their existence. For a start, people like this enable the rest of us to feel pleasantly superior while giving us all the opportunity to say 'woodenhead', which is a great word that should be used more often.

A young lady was standing next to her car in a shopping-centre car park, obviously distraught and crying. A passer-by stopped to ask her what the problem was, and was curious to hear the girl explain the batteries had gone flat on the remote-control locking device on her key fob. She had been trying to get into her car for an hour and finally decided she would have to take a taxi to the nearest dealership to have some new batteries fitted. At which point, the passer-by took the keys from her, manually unlocked the door and suggested she drive herself there, to save the expense of a taxi.

A middle-aged lady was at the supermarket check-out packing her things into bags as the cashier ran them through the bar-code scanner. Finally the shop assistant picked up the plastic divider, placed on the belt to separate customer purchases, and looked all over it for a bar code. Eventually she asked the customer if she knew how much the item was priced at. The lady just looked at the cashier and, with a completely straight face, replied, 'Oh, I have changed my mind, I don't want that now.' The cashier muttered that it was the third time that morning and placed the divider with the others on the shelf beside her.

A new secretary working for an insurance firm turned to a colleague on her first day and asked where she could find more paper in order to print out a document she had been typing. She was told to use paper from the photocopier so took the last plain sheet she had and made ten blank copies of it to refill her own printer.

Working at a branch of a well-known high-street bank, an employee telephoned the central IT support centre and said, 'I have smoke coming out of the back of my terminal. Do you have a fire in your office or something?'

In the summer of 1975, three men, on their way to rob a branch of a well-known Scottish bank, found themselves trapped in the revolving door. Members of staff released them and they left the building. Five minutes later, they returned and announced their intention of robbing the bank. The head cashier, who had helped free them from the door, burst out laughing, thinking he was on the receiving end of a practical joke. Disheartened, the ruthless gang reduced their demand from £5,000 to £500 and all the cashiers rolled about laughing. Finally the gang demanded £50 and, angered by the uncontrollable laughter of the bank staff, one of them leaped over the counter, breaking his leg in the process. His comedy colleagues then fled in panic, once again becoming trapped in the revolving door, which is where the police found them when they arrived.

In America, a man, pretending to have a gun, forced a motorist to drive to three separate cash points and proceeded to use his own card to withdraw money from his own account, before fleeing on foot, leaving a stunned driver scratching his head.

In Holland, a man tried to rob a local supermarket but was disappointed to find the takings were very low. With that, he tied up the shop assistant and worked on the tills himself, until the shop owner turned up three hours later and called the police.

In London, police were conducting an identity parade with a witness pacing along the line. Police asked the first person in the line-up to shout the words, 'Give me all the money or I will shoot!' at which point the suspect blurted out, 'But that isn't what I said.'

*

Down in Wales, a young man used the old favourite finger-in-the-jacket-pocket to indicate he had a gun when attempting to rob a late-night pharmacy. Wearing a balaclava, he demanded to be given the contents of the till and as the pharmacist hesitated, he pulled his gloved hand out and pointed his finger to the head of the pharmacist. 'If you don't hand it over, I will shoot!' he cried. 'With your finger?' the pharmacist asked, at which point the desperate criminal looked at his hand and muttered, 'Oh, shit!' before running out of the shop. A passing police car gave chase and the man was caught.

However, lawyers successfully argued that a charge of armed robbery should be dropped, as a finger is not a dangerous weapon. Charges of attempted robbery with the threat of force were later made.

My personal favourite is the tale of a South African man who was arrested after neighbours heard a series of gunshots in the garage of his house. Arresting officers asked for an explanation and the householder took them to the garage. There they found his car with seven bullet holes in the bonnet and windscreen. The man explained he had been having problems with the vehicle for months and so had decided to 'put it out of its misery'. He was charged with discharging his gun in a dangerous manner and spent three nights in jail before being bailed. Unrepentant, the man told local reporters the car had 'outlived its usefulness'. Although he admitted it was a 'stupid' thing to do he said he had no regrets. 'Every man in the universe has wanted to do that,' he explained. 'It was worth every minute in jail.' The part I like most about this story is the way he claims to speak for everybody to justify his stupidity. I, for one, have never wanted to shoot my car (although I've been known to threaten this computer with grievous bodily harm on occasion). Poetic justice would have given us a bulletproof windscreen on the car and a fatal ricochet.

The Cruel Hand of Fate

Next up come a couple of true stories that are more unfortunate than plain daft. First is the tale of how police hunting a well-known escaped convict had a stroke of luck when the man was admitted to hospital with appendicitis in the German city of Beuel. After his operation he was placed in a ward next to a man who was also recovering from an operation. Unknown to the convict, however, his neighbour was a policeman who was part of the team trying to track him down. Of course, he immediately recognized the criminal and sent his colleagues, who had been hunting the man for three months, a text message and the criminal was quickly rearrested and moved to the prison hospital.

Another example of how Fate likes to pull a fast one on us from time to time is the story, reported by a New Zealand newspaper, of how a fire that had destroyed a property had been traced by investigators to an electrical fault in a newly installed fire-detection alarm system. The distraught owner, unaware he was saying anything funny, commented to reporters, 'This is even worse than last year when someone broke in and stole my new security alarm system.'

The Wrong Car

Then there is the report of an elderly American lady who returned to her car with her bags to find four young males sitting in the vehicle. Not one to be messed with, she dropped her bags, took out her handgun and screamed that she knew how to use it and was prepared to if they didn't get out of the car. The four youngsters wisely didn't wait to find out and quickly scarpered. Witnesses watched in amazement as the old lady then took out her keys and tried to open the boot to put her shopping bags inside. Unfortunately the key didn't fit and the confused lady thought about it for a few moments, looked around and spotted her own identical car parked in a bay a few spaces along.

With that, she loaded her shopping and drove straight to the local police station to explain what had happened. Sitting in a room nearby were four pale and shaken youths reporting a car-jacking by a crazy, armed old lady. Luckily everybody saw the funny side and no charges were made.

MAKING YOUR OWN ENTERTAINMENT

Chicken Choker

A lady in Fulham, west London, had invited her girlfriends around on a Saturday night for a homemade curry and a lazy evening watching TV. When she checked her refrigerator, she noticed the chicken breasts were a few days past their sell-by date but decided to go ahead and cook them, thinking the meat was unlikely to give them all salmonella poisoning. But, just to be on the safe side, she decided to feed a slice to her cat and then keep an eye on its reaction. All seemed well and the group of friends enjoyed their meal, but when the lady went back to the kitchen it was to find the cat choking in the corner, in apparent seizure. She hurried back to her friends to explain what had happened and advised them all to attend the local Chelsea and Westminster Hospital and have their stomachs pumped, which they hastily did. In the meantime, the lady took her beloved pet straight to the nearest vet and was soon advised: 'Your cat is perfectly fine; she just had a fur ball lodged in her throat.' This story has been told at dinner parties for decades and has even appeared as a scene, featuring a poisoned casserole, in the 1989 Hollywood movie *Her Alibi*. In Britain it was also famously repeated in the 'rat poison and health inspector' scene in the classic comedy series *Fawlty Towers*, starring John Cleese.

Frozen Lips

Jenna is a university student and quite capable of keeping pace in the drinking games that form most of a university education these days. But after the events of New Year's Eve she has resolved to curb her enthusiasm in future. Walking back across campus at 3 a.m. on that cold night she was urged by her friends to simulate oral sex on a brass statue of a naked Greek god in the centre of the town square. Her friends all steadied their camera phones for the stunt but Jenna realized that as soon as her lips closed around the frosty member they had stuck fast. She was trapped with part of a Greek god in her mouth. She didn't even know his name, although that was nothing new, and her friends all howled with laughter as more and more passing students gathered to take pictures. Jenna's humiliation was complete as others removed her top to make an even better photograph and it took the campus security guard, who had been watching the whole event on CCTV, to rescue her with a flask of warm water poured over her face, defrosting the statue and releasing poor Jenna. Within days, there wasn't a single student who had not been sent 'Jenna: The Movie'. The statue? Well, he was smirking for weeks.

Stuck in Bed

A drunk was making his way home after a long night in the local pub when he took a wrong turn and found himself in an area of town he did not recognize. Confused and tired, he decided to jump over a fence into a children's playground before settling down on what he thought was soft grass to sleep off his ale. Unfortunately for him, he was not sleeping on soft grass but freshly laid cement on a new pathway. By the time he awoke, he was set fast and unable to move until workmen arrived and chiselled him out in the morning.

Sucking His Nuts

An elderly gentleman was in hospital recovering from a minor operation when he was visited by one of the young nurses. As they sat chatting, the man offered the girl some peanuts. She ate them all and then nibbled through another bowlful before announcing she had to leave to finish her rounds. As she stood up, the old man offered her the rest of the bag but she politely refused, as they were all that he had left. 'No really, take them,' he insisted. 'I don't like the peanuts so I just suck the chocolate off them instead.'

The Drunken Sailor

During the early 1900s, Major and Mrs Haversham bought a hundred-year-old farmhouse on the edge of the New Forest. The major, a keen collector of wine and spirits, was intrigued to find a 112-gallon oak barrel tucked away in the corner of the cellar. On testing the contents, he discovered the barrel was full of the finest naval rum. Experts agreed the unusually dark rum had benefited from years of ageing in the old oak barrel and was among the finest they had ever tasted.

The rum became the toast of the village, with neighbours and friends often celebrating national events at gatherings held at the Havershams' farmhouse. After five years, the major decided to decant what remained of the rum into a new smaller barrel and his wife suggested cutting the old one in half to use as containers for flowers on either side of their front door. However, when the workman employed to carry out the task opened up the barrel he found inside the perfectly preserved body of an eighteenth-century sailor.

It is well documented that when ordinary sailors died at sea they were stitched into their hammocks and thrown overboard. However, officers were often preserved in rum for the return journey before being buried on land with full naval honours. Lord Nelson's body was famously preserved in this way and brought back from Trafalgar for burial. (This is, incidentally, where the expression 'tapping the admiral' comes from, referring to a shot of some strong drink.) Therefore, as unlikely as this story seems, it is entirely possible that, after many months at sea, any large ship being unloaded could easily have had a few barrels of rum stolen and sold on the black market to a buyer unaware of the 'old salt' flavouring of one or two of them.

More People Vote for *Pop Idol* than for a General Election

The year 2002 saw the birth of the nation's obsession with music-based reality television programmes in the shape of *Pop Idol*. The programme was the first of many to introduce completely unknown, amateur singers trying their hand at established and popular songs in what was essentially a nationwide pub karaoke competition, televised live on a Saturday night. Personally I would rather lie in an empty bath with cold water dripping on my forehead for two hours than watch somebody I don't know destroy one of my favourite songs. But I appear to be in the minority as *Pop Idol* claims to attract over 32 million voters, which is six million more than the number of people who voted during the 2001 UK election. So, on the face of it, this myth appears to be true, although it comes as no surprise to find such apathy among the electorate as more people realize that if voting actually changed anything then we would not be allowed to do it. However, it doesn't take long to find holes in the myth. For a start, anybody can vote more than once for their pop idol and most people do. Then we learn that the estimated 32 million votes are cast over the duration of the twenty-week series and only ten million actually during the final programme. We can also assume that most of the people voting are probably children, students and council tax dodgers who are not listed on the electoral register anyway and therefore do not qualify to vote for the government.

But the popularity of reality television shows appears to be increasing and even now we have one that seems to be made up of uninteresting and bored people sitting around in a room watching a group of strangers doing exactly the same thing in the *Big Brother* house. So, the next time somebody tells you *Pop Idol* attracted more votes than the general election, do what I do. Give a big yawn and wander off to find somebody interesting to talk to.

Follow that Fish

Still on the subject of television, BBC documentary makers were compiling a series for television about Scottish wildlife and were preparing a programme about the lifecycle of wild salmon. Having decided to trace the movements of a wild salmon over a six-month period, the producers caught one of the younger fish and inserted an electronic chip complete with tracking device so that they could monitor its movements over a period of time. Everything went well for a while and the team became excited as the season changed and the fish began its journey back upstream towards fresh water in order to breed. They carefully monitored progress and were delighted at how the documentary was turning out to be one of the best they had filmed. However, one afternoon, the young naturalist who was operating the tracking monitor noticed the beacon suddenly veer away from the river at right angles. They quickly sent a crew to trail the signal and within minutes stumbled across a campsite for Boy Scouts. And there, sizzling away on a barbecue, was the star of their latest wildlife documentary.

Nobby's Nails

This leads on to a legend I am certain is untrue but it still makes a good story. In Australia (although the story has also been set in America, Africa and Europe), a well-known nail and screw manufacturer called Nobby's Nails had decided on a new advertising campaign. The owners of the company were a particularly religious family, well known for employing only those who shared their beliefs. As a result, the instructions to their advertising agency were that they wanted a religious feel to the campaign, and this had proved to be a problem for the usually creative company. However, one particularly bright spark felt he had solved the dilemma and the new advert was created. On the Sunday it was to be first aired, the managing director invited all of his fellow churchgoers over to his house for lunch and to watch the national screening of the advert on TV. In the first shot was a magnificent scene depicting Jesus standing on a hilltop looking out across the plain. Then, on seeing two figures on the horizon, he turns and starts to run. The scene then switches to two Roman centurions running along, and one turns to the other and says, 'I told you, this would never have happened if we'd used Nobby's Nails.' It can't be true, can it?

Happy Birthday to You

Everybody, the world over, knows the song 'Happy Birthday to You'. It has been one of the most popular and frequently sung melodies in the English-speaking world for over a hundred years. The song forms the centrepiece of every birthday party; it is used in musicals, birthday cards and ring tones, reproduced in just about every medium one can imagine. And there can be no doubt it will continue to be used for the rest of time. 'Happy Birthday to You', like Father Christmas, seems to have been around for ever. Which is why it surprises everybody to find out that, in fact just like Father Christmas himself (see the next entry), this little song with its six-note melody and simple lyrics is protected by copyright. That means somebody owns it and every time it is used, commercially at least, it should be paid for. Which would make the songwriter even richer than Paul McCartney, if the person was still alive of course. But who wrote it?

The tale of the 'Happy Birthday' song leads us to two sisters by the names of Patty and Mildred Smith. Patty, born in 1868, started out as a Sunday school teacher, then later developed a system of education called the 'Patty Hill Blocks' and became a key founder of the National Association for the Education of Young Children. Her sister Mildred, born in 1859, also started her career as a Sunday school teacher but took a musical direction, becoming a concert pianist, organist and composer. One day, in 1893, while teaching at Patty's Louisville Experimental Kindergarten School, she came up with a simple little melody which Patty then wrote some words to:

> Good morning to you.
> Good morning to you.
> Good morning, dear children.
> Good morning to all.

The song was used to greet the children in class every morning, and during that same year was included in the songbook *Song Stories for Kindergarten*, and while establishing a copyright in the process, it also proved to be an instant hit, with different variations on the lyrics. For example, students would reverse the greeting:

> Good morning to you.
> Good morning to you.
> Good morning, dear teacher.
> Good morning to you.

Other variations, such as 'Good Night' and 'Happy Greetings', also became popular. Nobody knows who included the words 'Happy Birthday', but in 1924 the lyrics first appeared in a songbook edited by Richard H. Coleman, and by the mid 1930s the melody was widely used in radio and films, with versions appearing on stage in the Broadway musicals *Bandwagon* in 1931, *Singing Telegram* in 1933 and Irving Berlin's *As Thousands Cheer* of the same year. However, no credit was made to the Smiths for its use. And it was at this point a third sister, Jessica Hill, who administered her sisters' copyright, filed a lawsuit for breach. She was easily able to demonstrate the similarities between 'Good Morning to You' and 'Happy Birthday to You' to the High Court and secured the copyright of 'Happy Birthday' in 1934. It was the Chicago music publisher Clayton F. Summy who published and copyrighted 'Happy Birthday' for a 28-year term that was then renewed for a similar length of time. But the Copyright Act of 1976 extended the term of all copyrights to seventy-five years from the date of publication, and the Copyright Term Extension Act of 1998 added a further twenty years, resulting in the copyright of 'Happy Birthday' remaining secured until 2030.

But don't worry if you want to sing 'Happy Birthday' to little Johnny at his party next week because you will not have to pay for private performance rights. It is only commercial use that requires a licence and needs to be paid for although, technically speaking, if singing in a public place such as a restaurant, pub or club, you will need to contact ASCAP or the Harry Fox Agency for permission. Nobody has ever been prosecuted in such a case and I doubt anybody ever will be. That would hardly be in the spirit of the Smith family, would it? It is often rumoured Paul McCartney now owns the copyright to 'Happy Birthday' and I imagine he wishes he does but, although his company MPL Communications is one of the world's largest owners of music copyright, 'Happy Birthday' is not in their song catalogue.

In the late 1930s, a New York accountant called John F. Sengstack acquired the Clayton F. Summy company and later relocated the firm to New Jersey, renaming it Birch Tree Ltd. During the 1970s, Warner Chappell, a division of Warner Communications, paid a reported $25 million for Birch Tree Ltd, again changing its name, to Summy Birchard Music this time. David Sengstack, the company chairman, claims 'Happy Birthday' still accrues $2 million a year in royalties, and the proceeds are divided between Summy Birchard and the Hill Foundation, once administered by Archibald Hill, Jessica's son, who inherited 'Happy Birthday' from his aunts in 1935. At that time, he was the professor of English at the University of Virginia, where he remained until 1952. He retired in 1972, publishing many acclaimed essays and books on linguistics before he finally died in 1992 at home in Austin, Texas. As a song, 'Happy Birthday to You' became a worldwide phenomenon and has become more popular every year since it was written in 1893. Even McCartney cannot compete with that, yet.

Santa Claus is the Real Thing

Children throughout the world look forward to Christmas and the appearance of the little fat man in his red suit and jolly white beard. Santa tribute acts have appeared at children's parties, private homes and shopping centre grottos for as long as most of us can remember, firmly establishing Christmas as just about the most important part of the year for anybody under twelve years old. Most, if not all, of us have tried to stay awake long enough to see Rudolph clip-clopping across the rooftops bringing Santa to our chimneys. And then, as we get a little older and realize we don't have a chimney, to catch Mum or Dad munching Rudolph's carrot and Granny downing Santa's sherry or mince pie.

European folklore has included stories of the mysterious Yuletide gift-giver based on the legend of St Nicholas, a former bishop of Asia Minor, since the fourth century BC. But in truth it

was the Dutch who first introduced the idea of Santa Claus as the bringer of a sack full of gifts at Christmas on board his sleigh, drawn by eight reindeer all the way from his home at the North Pole. They called this fellow Sante Klaas and carol singers often accompanied him. This image spread quickly through America as that newly independent country struggled to establish its own traditions in the eighteenth century. Then along came Clement C. Moore and Thomas Nast. It was Moore who, in 1823, published his poem 'A Visit from St Nicholas' (better known as ''Twas the Night Before Christmas'), describing Santa as a jolly little fat man with a white beard:

His eyes – how they twinkled! His dimples how
merry!
His cheeks were like roses, his nose like a cherry;
His droll little mouth was drawn up like a bow,
And the beard on his chin was as white as the
snow . . .
He had a broad face, a little round belly
That shook when he laughed, like a bowl of jelly.
He was chubby and plump, a right jolly elf . . .

Later, in 1863 as the Civil War raged, the
political cartoonist Thomas Nast was asked to
create a version of St Nicholas for *Harper's
Illustrated Weekly*. Nast reproduced Moore's
Santa in a now-famous image of him as a happy
plump elf wearing a woolly suit with whiskers
and a beard handing out gifts to soldiers and
their children. But he still doesn't look quite
like our Santa; in fact he is wearing a Stars and
Stripes jacket.

For our now accepted image of Santa Claus,
we need to travel back to the late nineteenth
century and the invention of Coca-Cola, a popular new 'medicinal' drink containing coca bean
extract (cocaine), which guaranteed a renewed
vitality and agility while in the process generally
making you feel good. No surprise there then.
Coca-Cola was usually available as an adult
pick-me-up down at any local pharmacy, but by
1930 the company had decided to broaden the
drink's appeal as something for the whole family.

Cocaine had been replaced by caffeine, but sales during the Depression were slow and a new marketing plan was called for.

In 1931, Coca-Cola launched an extensive new advertising campaign that pioneered the use of well-known artists to create images for their product to be used for nationwide sales promotions. The most successful of these images was produced by a Swedish artist called Haddon Sundblom, who, modelling Santa on retired salesman Lou Prentice, portrayed him as a jolly little fat man with a white beard, red suit and hat, handing out bottles of Coke to families at Christmas. This was when the modern image of Santa Claus first appeared and remains a Coca-Cola image to this day, which is why you never see Santa Claus featured in any other advert. They own the image and no one else is allowed to recreate it for their use. That's right, kids: Coca-Cola owns Santa.

Sundblom's creation is now the accepted worldwide image of Father Christmas and must go down as one of the most successful marketing campaigns of all time which, happily, has led to a down side. The fact that the Santa image is so well known – more so, in some parts of the world, than even Coca-Cola – means that most people do not associate the two in any way at all. I believe the expression is 'hoist by their own petard'.

THE APPLIANCE OF SCIENCE

The Chicken Test

One of the oldest and best-loved urban legends tells the story of a major manufacturer of aircraft windscreens. On one occasion, as they were performing tests to establish impact resistance, a young trainee was asked to carry out the 'high-velocity bird' experiment and was told the procedure meant he had to go to the local supermarket and buy a chicken. Then he should return to the testing centre and fire the bird directly at the glass windscreen at 800 miles per hour using a specially constructed testing rig. Once the young scientist had set up the test, the observers were all called in to monitor the results and were horrified to see the chicken not only smash through the windscreen but travel another forty yards and pierce the metal wall of the warehouse.

The designers had to rethink their ideas and it took another six months before the experiment could be repeated. The next time they were fully

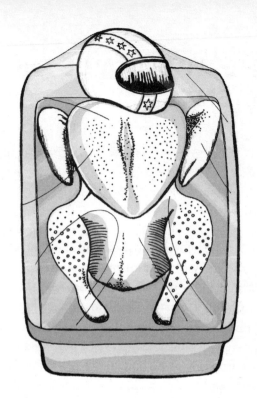

confident and a journalist asked, before the test was carried out, what changes they had made to the windscreen design. 'Nothing,' replied the company spokesman, 'only this time we are making sure the chicken has been defrosted.' I would love this story to be true, but the reality is that, in such a high-tech industry as aircraft design, it is unthinkable that such experiments would be so rudimentary. At least, I prefer to believe that.

Musical Breasts

It has been reported that tiny computer chips used for storing and cataloguing music, like the ones used in many personal music systems, could soon be included in women's breast implants. Effectively one breast could hold an MP3 player or iPod and the other an entire music collection in what would appear to be some sort of mammary memory board. It is claimed that BT's Foresight and Futurology Unit is currently developing the idea, which, they say, should be available within fifteen years. According to them, silicone gel, used to make implants, can easily be developed for light computing tasks. BT Laboratories analyst Ian Pearson is quoted as explaining how a flexible plastic electronic panel could sit inside the breast, relaying signals to a pair of headphones and controlled via Bluetooth on a wristband. He was quoted in the *Sun* as saying, 'It is now very hard for me to think of breast implants as just decorative. If a woman has to have something permanently implanted, then it may as well do something useful.'

It remains to be seen how the idea will develop, but already I can imagine young men excusing their misbehaviour by using the old 'I am just scrolling down to find your Beatles album or my favourite Rolling Stones track' argument in their

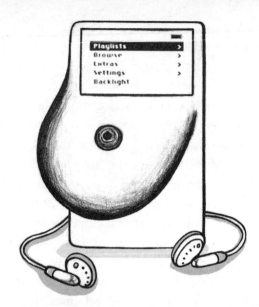

Playlists
Browse
Extras
Settings
Backlight

defence. Or how long will it be before divorce cases are being heard where the next-door neighbour claims he was only listening to the news headlines, in stereo.

In a more serious vein, using such technology would also apparently make it possible to warn of heart murmurs, increases in blood pressure and impending illness such as breast cancer or diabetes. Ian Pearson suggests all sorts of technology could be developed in this way, including mobile telephones and PDAs, and that the future for breasts is indeed a bright one. Which is fantastic news, because I have always been a big fan.

While on that subject, I am reminded of an apparently true story published in the eminent

Recent research has proved that prolonged staring at ladies' breasts can increase the length of a man's life. Personally I think it depends on which lady as I expect there might be some circumstances where it could instead reduce it, down to just a few minutes if you weren't careful. After lengthy research, the gerontologist Dr Karen Weatherby has announced that 'just ten minutes of staring at the charms of a well-endowed female is roughly equivalent to a thirty-minute aerobic work-out'. This genius of a doctor and her fellow researchers at three hospitals in Frankfurt, Germany, have reached their conclusions after considering the health of 200 male outpatients, half of whom were tasked with looking at busty ladies every day while the other half were told not to do so. Five long years of study revealed the lecherous legion to have lower blood pressure, slower resting pulse rates and fewer cases of coronary artery disease.

'Sexual excitement gets the heart pumping,' explained Dr Weatherby in what must be an Olympic medal-winning example of stating the bleeding obvious. 'That improves blood circulation,' she continued. 'There is no question gazing at breasts makes men healthier. Our study indicates that engaging in this activity for a few minutes a day cuts the risk of stroke and heart attacks in half. We believe that by doing so consistently, the average man can extend his life by four to five years.' (Not being the average man, I have just calculated that by this reckoning I am to live until I am 345 years old and will never need to go to the gym, which is even greater news.)

Just Take It Back!

This is the transcript of a PC manufacturer's new sales helpline operator in conversation with a customer who had been having a spot of bother with a new computer.

'Good evening, this is Damon. How can I help you?'

'Well, I am having a little trouble with this new PC your company sold me.'

'What appears to be the problem?'

'I was working away quite happily in the Word programme, when the words I was writing suddenly disappeared.'

'I see. Had you backed the file up before this happened?'

'Backed it up – you mean like reversing it?'

'No, I mean, like, did you save what you'd written before you lost it?'

'No.'

'Oh dear, well let's see if we can try to find it for you. What can you see on your screen now?'

'Nothing.'

'Nothing at all?'

'No, it's completely blank.'

'Can you even see your desktop?'

'Yes, I can see that.'

'Well, try clicking on the little symbol for the Word file on the screen and open it again.'

'I told you, it's completely blank. There's nothing there.'

'But you said you could see your desktop?'

'I can.'

'What can you see on it?'

'My computer, the phone and a mug of tea?'

'Ah, I see, that desktop. OK, let's try this another way. Does your monitor have the power light on?'

'What is the monitor?'

'The screen in front of you that looks like a TV. Are there any small red or green lights on your computer anywhere?'

'No.'

'OK, is the power cable still plugged into the back of the PC?'

'Hang on, I'll reach over the back – yes it is.'

'OK, is the other end plugged into the wall?'

'Yes, it is. Look, I'm not that stupid!'

'OK, OK, I'm just going through all the checks. Is the cable between the back of the screen and the rest of the computer plugged in securely?'

'I don't know, I can't reach round there.'

'OK, but if you kneel on the desk can you at least see if it is plugged in securely and not only half in or something like that?'

'Can you hang on? I will have to get a torch.'

'A torch?'

'Yes, the only light I have on is coming in through the window.'

'Can't you turn the room light on?'

'No, we've just had a power cut.'

'A power . . . a power cut? OK, we have got this sorted out now. Do you still have the boxes, manuals and a receipt?'

'Yes, they are all here. I only bought it yesterday.'

'Good, that's good. You need to put everything back in the box, exactly as it came, and take it all back to the shop with the receipt.'

'Oh no, is it really that bad?'

'Yes, I am afraid it is that bad.'

'OK, what shall I tell them when I get there?'

'Well, ask for your money back. Just tell them that you really are too stupid to own a computer after all.'

Click.

Millennium Buggery

In 1999, many people believed an all-powerful computer bug was going to invade their computers, destroy their files, bank accounts and business records, bring every aeroplane crashing to the ground, and swallow their children. This theoretical monster was known as the Y2K or Millennium Bug. We were told that all critical businesses, such as the financial sector or electronics industry, would stop working at 12 a.m.

precisely on 1 January 2000. Media speculation, corporate and government reports proliferated and companies all over the world spent millions on consultants to help protect their computing networks and upgrade their systems. Imagine that: the great minds of the world spending money on getting other great minds to come round and stop their systems being devoured by a creepy crawly, albeit of a spooky electronic kind. I didn't understand any of it but I managed to back up all my files, pulled all the plugs out of the walls and drew the sheets over my head until I could hear people moving around outside a few days later. I figured if they were all OK still, it must be safe to get out of bed.

It all began in 1995 when computer software programmers began to discuss Century Date Change (CDC) and Faulty Date Logic (FADL) and speculation began that programmes store years as only two digits, meaning the year 2000 would be shown as 00. The fear was that this might be interpreted by software as 1900, causing critical infrastructures to fail, and contingency planning became the buzz phrase. In case you are wondering, no, I don't know what all these words mean, but fortunately minds immeasurably greater than mine were at work and during the late 1990s millions of lines of programming code were altered and updated, and in fact the turning of the millennium went without a single hitch after all.

But to investigate further, I have just spoken to a computing expert by the name of John Riley who told me, using complicated technical language (and I quote): 'That was a load of old bollocks!' According to him, it was just a bunch of clever people worrying about very little and a bunch of other people cleverer than them making a shedload of cash out of it. So I asked him if there had been, in his opinion, a very real problem during the 1990s that had been identified and then put right in time, and he replied that he very much doubted it.

It has been estimated that in the end US$300 billion was spent in preparation for the Millennium Bug, but in the event the only problems reported included an Australian bus ticket machine failing to work and a French weather map displaying the wrong date. The question is this: was it worth spending all that money? There is no way of knowing, however, as the people the money was spent on will argue they fixed all the problems in time and saved the planet. There's no price on that, is there? On the other hand, some maintain that there were no critical problems after all and the supporting evidence for this is the lack of Millennium Bug problems experienced in the Third World and other countries who spent very little on the situation. I am coming down on the side of our expert Mr Riley and believe we may have all been shafted. I suspect Millennium Buggery.

Fatal Tan

A young lady had been looking forward to her wedding day for months. During that time the couple had been preparing for the event, and as the day drew nearer the lady booked a series of sunbed sessions down at her local salon. The wedding went perfectly and she looked healthy and radiant in all of the wedding photographs. On the first day of the honeymoon, however, the new bride dropped dead, without any warning. The autopsy report revealed her internal organs had been slow-cooked by a faulty sunbed.

This story can't be true, of course, as it suggests that a sunbed can operate like a microwave oven. The fact is that the ultra violet rays emitted from a sunbed, just like UV rays in sunlight, cannot penetrate human skin and are therefore completely harmless to the internal organs of the body. The effect on the skin is another matter, however, regular sunbed users being easily recognized by their leathery, years-older-looking complexions.

The End of Life as We Know It (Again)

Towards the tail end of 2005, a scientific conference dedicated to security in the event of comet and asteroid attack (yes, this type of conference does take place) was held at the Practical Astronomy Institute of the Russian Academy of Sciences in St Petersburg. Within days, the Russian media were reporting that scientist Viktor Shor, of the Institute, had claimed that many experts could see a real threat of the 2004 MN4 asteroid colliding with Earth in the year 2028, wiping out life on the planet.

Experts from the Russian Institute of Calculus Mathematics and Mathematical Physics also provided scale models of asteroid-induced tsunami waves to demonstrate the impact of an asteroid on the ocean, causing waves several hundred metres high. Earthquake-induced tsunami waves rarely exceed fifty metres in height. The models illustrated that while the impact of a 500-metre asteroid, travelling at between ten and twenty kilometres an hour, would create waves 200 metres high, one measuring ten kilometres in diameter would cause waves up to five kilometres in height which would still be 300 metres high when they hit land. Scientists claim a similar disaster took place millions of years ago, at the time of the dinosaurs, which resulted in the extinction of 90 per cent of all living species.

Unsurprisingly, this report caused widespread panic and was the origin of a number of 'the world is about to end' rumours. Shor himself did little to dispel such fears when he claimed that his own subsequent research predicted that although by 2028 the 2004 MN4 asteroid would have changed its orbit and narrowly miss the Earth, it could well return seven years later to hit the bull's-eye. Ah, so that's OK then; no need to worry after all.

America's National Aeronautics and Space Administration (NASA), whose Near-Earth Object Programme is monitoring the threat, state publicly that although the 512-kilometre-wide 2004 MN4 asteroid will pass close enough to Earth to be visible to the naked eye, their current risk analysis for 2004 MN4 indicates that 'no subsequent Earth encounters in the twenty-first century are of concern'. But then they would say that, wouldn't they?

One Thousand Miles Per Gallon

A story has been reported in America of a driver who noticed that the fuel gauge of his new car had barely moved, despite him driving more than 2,000 miles in the first week. Puzzled by this, and expecting the gauge to be faulty, he returned the car to the dealer, explaining the problem. The manager immediately offered to take the car back, saying he would be happy to give the customer more than the original price for it. Highly suspicious about all this, the driver refused. It was later revealed he had inadvertently been sold an experimental model by mistake. The car manufacturer had developed an engine that used hardly any fuel and was able to drive for more than one thousand miles on a single gallon of petrol. The oil industry, desperate to keep the invention a secret, had paid billions of pounds to the engine maker to buy the patent and then lock the new technology away for ever. Eventually the customer was paid a huge cash bonus and given a new car every year for life in return for the experimental car and a confidentiality agreement.

Global Warming: We Are All Going to Drown

Yet another warning about global warming comes along, accompanied by calls from environmental activists to cut down on emissions and ban cars and all aeroplanes. In fact, we must turn off all our electricity and go and live in a hut for ever. But that is what it is like in parts of central Africa today, and it is no cooler there than it is here, I can assure you. I was looking out of my window when I heard the latest report and, with it being about minus three degrees outside, I thought I could do with a bit of global warming myself.

It is fair to say that, with any belief system, extremist elements will emerge. So how long will it be, then, before the Extreme Green movement appears, a modern-day version of General Ned Ludd's Army of Redressers who attempted to prevent the Industrial Revolution in the early 1800s by using force and terrorism against all new technology? The Luddite movement ended in 1817, with twenty-three executions and thirteen men being transported to Australia for life, but just you try explaining that to the Green movement today. Global warming, we are told, will result in the polar ice caps breaking up, sea levels rising and, as a result, millions of people drowning in fifty years' time. But I won't drown. I won't be standing on the coastline waiting for the water to reach the top of my wellington boots; I will simply walk uphill for a few yards. And so too, I imagine, will everybody else.

Wondering if I could dispel this persistent myth, I found out, as anyone else can for him or herself, that our climate warms and cools all the time, quite naturally. While there are periods of global warming, we also have global cooling from time to time. True, our human activities can add what are known as 'greenhouse gases' to the atmosphere and that can produce a warming effect. But it is important to put this into some sort of context. The great ice age began a million years ago and reached its zenith 80,000 years later. As recently as 6,000 years ago, Canada was still covered in ice and parts of it still are. It has taken 20,000 years for the sun to melt the ice and, although both polar ice caps, all that remain from that period, are also slowly but surely melting away, resulting in more icebergs, to blame this on air travel and a few big cars with heavy carbon dioxide emissions seems a little ridiculous to me. American satellite monitoring has not shown any warming of the atmosphere since studies began in 1979, and while most scientists 'guess' human activity may have some effect on our atmosphere, it will be tiny in comparison with the natural fluctuations of our climate. Even if any change at all is noticed, some scientists have been quoted as saying that while it may have 'some interesting scientific curiosity, it will have no practical importance at all'. There has also been no ozone-layer depletion since 1992.

Apparently the climate did heat up a little between 1880 and 1940 and that speeded up the current so-called break-up of the polar ice caps, which in fact means just a few more icebergs appearing as they split from the main body in the Arctic and Antarctic. But fear not, as the period between 1940 and 1975 was, once again, a cooling period, the effects of which are likely to be felt during the later part of this century. So it seems that despite all the efforts of the scaremongers and activists, none of us are going to be drowned by global warming as this process has been going on for around a million years and may still have 10,000 years to go. I can think of many more ways we will ruin the planet than with the cars we drive or the aerosols we use. Many even believe that the increase in carbon dioxide in our atmosphere will be a good thing, especially for agriculture that thrives in such conditions, and crops will grow stronger and more reliably. And finally, the Earth's own climate creates natural filters. For example, if the sea heats up, more water vapour is created, causing more evaporation, which produces more clouds, which prevents the sun's rays from reaching the earth's surface. And that, in turn, cools the planet down again.

In 1997, a global warming agreement was written in Kyoto, Japan, proposing limits on greenhouse gases that would 'harm the environment, hinder the advance of science and technology and damage the health and welfare of mankind'. But over 20,000 qualified scientists signed the following petition in response: 'We urge the United States government to reject the global warming agreement written in Kyoto, Japan, in December 1997 and any other similar proposals. The proposed limits on greenhouse gases would harm the environment, hinder the advance of science and technology and damage the health and welfare of mankind.'

There is no convincing scientific evidence that human release of carbon dioxide, methane, or other greenhouse gases is causing or will, in the foreseeable future, cause catastrophic heating of the Earth's atmosphere and disruption of the Earth's climate. Moreover, there is substantial scientific evidence that increases in atmospheric carbon dioxide produce many beneficial effects upon the natural world.

The United States Government never did sign the Kyoto Agreement. Ruin the planet we probably will, although not in our lifetime and not through global warming, which is a shame because it is still freezing in here. In fact it might even be snowing in my bathroom.

Can We Digest Chewing Gum?

The common belief is that chewing gum, or bubble gum, takes seven years to digest if it is swallowed. Generally, parents encourage their children not to swallow gum as it is indigestible and the stomach could soon fill up with seven years' worth of gum, leading to illness or even death. The truth is that chewing gum is made up of five basic ingredients: corn syrup, softeners, sweeteners, flavouring and a synthetic or rosin-derived gum base that forms the chewy part. The first four ingredients dissolve in the mouth but the gum base does not. Instead it retains the same size and consistency for however long it is chewed. If this part is swallowed, it will not be broken down and digested, but it does not stay in the stomach for seven years: it will be passed out through the body's waste system within two days. So while it is not advisable to swallow anything that cannot be digested, including gum base, the latter will not do any harm and will not lie in the stomach for seven years. Instead, most of it ends up on the sole of my shoe after being spat out.

One Small Step for Man . . .

Much has been made in the past of the Apollo moon landings, which took place between 1969 and 1972, and conspiracy theories have circulated ever since Neil Armstrong, Edwin 'Buzz' Aldrin and Michael Collins first landed their Saturn 5 craft. I also have my doubts when I look at the famous photo of the Lunar Module, astronaut and apparently fluttering US flag. For a start, we know there is no atmosphere on the moon, so where does the wind come from? Also, the light, shadows and lack of visible stars are suspicious, and we can see the moon's surface clearly and it certainly doesn't look like cheese to me. Some people insist the whole thing was

staged in a studio under the Nevada Desert, but if that were true, why have space observers all over the world, including Russia, which was certainly watching with interest, not revealed the hoax if it was one? So, in fact, we just don't know. We do know, however, that no moon landings have taken place since 1972, by America, Russia or anybody else, which invites the question – why not?

And what we also know is that Neil Armstrong, who was given the now-famous scripted speech to make from the moon surface, fluffed his lines. What Armstrong was given to recite was: 'That is one small step for a man – one giant leap for mankind,' but what he actually said was:

'That's one small step for man, one giant leap for mankind.' This has had English-language buffs and space nuts going for over thirty years. On the one hand, 'man' without the indefinite article 'a' in front of it has the same meaning as 'mankind'. This suggests Armstrong effectively said: 'That's one small step for mankind and one giant leap for mankind.' Space nuts, on the other hand, claim radio interference simply led to the 'a' not being heard properly. And who can be bothered to argue with them? Quite simply, moon landing or not, fluffed lines or not, it is quite probably the most famous sentence ever spoken, and there is no argument about who said it. It definitely was Neil Armstrong.

There is another story claiming Armstrong also uttered the cryptic line 'Good luck, Mr Gorsky' as he re-entered the Lunar Module. Many believed at the time Armstrong was making a reference to someone involved in the Russian space programme. However, extensive research failed to reveal anyone by that name and, when asked about it, Armstrong refused to answer. It is then claimed that on 5 July 1995, while he was answering questions following a speech made in Tampa, Florida, the question was put to Armstrong again, 'Who is Mr Gorsky?' This time, it is said, Armstrong announced that as the Gorskys had now passed away he could reveal the meaning of his cryptic message without embarrassing anybody. He then went on to tell the story of when he was a young boy playing baseball with his brother and had hit the ball into the garden of his neighbours, a Mr and Mrs Gorsky. As he went to retrieve it, he heard, through an open window, Mrs Gorsky yelling at her husband, 'Oral sex, you want oral sex. You can have that the day the kid next door walks on the moon!' Now that's a story I can believe!

Mobile Phones Will Rot Your Brain

We have long been told that radiation emissions from mobile phones will lead to a greater risk of getting cancer. First, the phone itself was the culprit, we were told. Then, after the introduction of hands-free earpieces, they became the problem, and finally the sites of mobile-network transmission aerials were deemed potential cancer hot spots. Such is the concern generated by this ongoing myth that studies are regularly commissioned, with none yet able to prove the link between mobile phone use and the increased incidence of brain tumours.

Mobile phones are extremely low-powered radio devices able to receive and transmit microwave radiation, which is why some people believe that holding one to your ear has the same effect as placing your head in a microwave oven. But information from the Health Protection

Agency's Radiation Protection Division states that 'radiowaves do not have sufficient energy to damage genetic material [DNA, to you and me] in cells and therefore cannot cause cancer'.

It appears the actual level of radiowave energy in the body caused by using a mobile phone can be measured and monitored. This is known as the Specific Absorption Rate (SAR) and every mobile phone is now sold with an SAR rating well within the international level guidelines, even though such a measure is not strictly necessary because radio waves cannot damage the body in any case. And while nearly all research concludes there is no danger, it is worth noting that most of the studies were carried out on analogue phones and the modern digital unit gives off even less radiowave radiation than its analogue predecessor.

In January 2006, a study of 2,500 people in the UK found no link at all between brain illness and mobile phones, although since most people have not been using mobile phones for more than fifteen years, the long-term consequences to health, if there are any, remain unknown. Yet there is also solid evidence that mobile phones can be good for you. Alan Preece, who studies the effects of mobile-phone radiation on the body at the University of Bristol, found that people exposed to mobile-phone radiation were approximately 4 per cent faster at performing certain mental tasks than others. Preece also claims that this radiation has the effect of making a person appear younger due to the phone heating a region of the brain called the cortex. Radiation from phones has also been shown to increase blood flow in certain regions of the brain.

It is believed, however, that carrying a mobile phone in a trouser pocket could lower a man's sperm count by as much as 30 per cent. The findings of Dr Imre Fejes, a scientist at the University of Szeged in Hungary, suggest that radiation from a phone kept either in a trouser pocket or hung from a belt can have an adverse effect on sperm count and the mobility of surviving sperm. My feeling is that most young men's sperm is quite mobile enough and, if the profusion of pushchairs and prams on any local high street is anything to go by, should be slowed down considerably more.

Dr Fejes has reported that the average sperm count of male mobile-phone users is around 59 million per millilitre of seminal fluid, compared to 83 million in the case of non-users. It is a conclusion that raises as many questions as it answers, such as how do some of these scientists choose their line of work and why?

So, while most studies conclude your brain is safe from mobile phones, it would appear, according to Dr Fejes, that our balls are still very much at risk. And nobody likes to hear that. My own conclusion is that these days we are all at far more risk of delinquent fifteen-year-olds kicking in our heads, or balls, and stealing the damn thing anyway.

Semen is Good for You

For many years, scientists have looked into the risks of having unprotected sex. On 26 June 2002, the *New Scientist* published an article that caught the attention of many entitled 'Semen Can Act as an Anti Depressant', which concluded that having unprotected sex makes you happy. Gordon Gallup, a psychologist at the State University of New York, led the study team and found that women who were directly exposed to semen were less depressed than those who used condoms because mood-altering hormones in male semen are absorbed into the female body.

In what must have been the jammiest piece of scientific research to have been involved in, Gallup's team divided 293 female students into groups depending how often their partners used condoms, and then assessed their levels of happiness using the Beck Depression Inventory, in which those with a points total of 17 are considered depressed. Survey results later revealed that women directly exposed to semen scored an average of 8 points while those who used condoms all the time scored around 15. Women having no sex at all scored 13.5 points. Gallup also found that cases of depression, suicide or attempted suicide were much higher among women who used condoms, and you have to admire his bravery in asking such a question of a depressed or suicidal lady: 'Please, miss, will you come down off that window ledge? Oh, and by the way, when you and your boyfriend have sex, do you use a condom?'

But Gallup is convinced: 'It suggests there is something in semen that can alter moods. If you could isolate what it is in semen that appears to be doing this, you might be able to use it as an alternative way of treating depression.' The survey also revealed women exposed to semen find they are able to recover from broken relationships more quickly. 'They experience rebound,' said Gallup. 'It is as if they find semen addictive.' Meanwhile, further evidence from the University of Adelaide suggests exposure to semen during pregnancy can strengthen the mother's immune system, thereby helping to protect the growing foetus.

I have no doubt many amateur scientists reading this are now about to carry out their own experiments – all in the name of scientific research, of course. But a word of advice: be very careful about introducing your semen to women who are hormonal or depressed. You have been warned.

Duct Tape Suffocation

In the wake of the terrorist attacks on 11 September 2001 there were several cases of anthrax, sarin or other poisonous substances being sent through the post. People in their heightened state of anxiety were worried about chemical attacks and many carried safety masks with them. In February 2003, the US Department of Homeland Security advised citizens to create what they called a 'safe area' in their homes by completely sealing certain rooms with plastic sheeting and duct tape in case of a chemical or biological attack in their town or city. Many followed this advice, but myths about people suffocating in their sleep spread across the country and questions were raised about the likelihood of dying in this way. But the truth is, it was not a myth at all: it did happen. The Associated Press reported in March 2003 that a woman and her two teenage sons had suffocated during the night at their home in Kfar Kassem, Israel. The region had been a dangerous place to live for many years, but with the War on Terror now being waged in nearby Iraq, many Israelis treated the threat of chemical or biological attack very seriously and created their own sealed 'safe' areas. The problem was that the family in question kept a coal-fuelled heater in the same room and the fire gradually sucked all the air from the room. At 5 a.m. the father of the family woke and soon realized his wife and two teenage sons were not breathing, although the couple's two younger children survived along with their father.

Duct tape was invented during the Second World War and, being both air- and waterproof, it was used by military personnel to seal ammunition cases. The tape was made using cotton duck, a fabric similar to that used in bandages, and as a result was initially called 'duck tape'. After the war it was used during the housing boom to connect heating and air conditioning ducts together, and that is when the name was corrupted and the tape became known, erroneously at first, as 'duct tape'.

The Locked-out Pilots

Passengers in the front seats of a commercial flight during the 1950s were reassured by both the captain and co-pilot coming to tell them that the plane was flying on the newly installed automatic navigation system. Passengers could see that the aircraft was flying consistently and were impressed by the new technology. That was until heavy turbulence not only altered the aircraft's course but also slammed shut the cockpit door. The frantic pilots and passengers had to break the door down with an axe before the captain could regain control of the flight.

THE BENEFITS OF HINDSIGHT: REMARKS MADE AND REGRETTED

The following are a series of true remarks made by people who would rather you didn't know about them.

'I think there is a world market for no more than five computers' – Thomas Watson, IBM Chairman, 1948.

'It will never catch on. Who would want to hear actors talk?' – H. M. Warner, Warner Brothers, 1927.

'Guitar music is on the way out' – Decca Records writing to Brian Epstein and rejecting The Beatles in 1962.

'Heavier-than-air flying machines are impossible' – Lord Kelvin, President of the Royal Society in 1895.

'Lesbian forces are moving down from the north towards Israel' – The BBC reporting on the Lebanese army.

'This, the greatest of all wars, is not just another war, it is the last war' – H. G. Wells on the First World War, 1914.

'The telephone has too many shortcomings to be seriously considered as a means of communication. The device is inherently of no value to us' – A Western Union internal memo in 1876.

'No woman in my time will be prime minister or chancellor or foreign secretary – none of the top jobs. I wouldn't want to be prime minister anyway' – Margaret Thatcher in 1969, ten years before becoming prime minister.

'Well, Mr President, you can't say the people of Dallas haven't given you a nice welcome' – Mrs John Connally only seconds before Kennedy was shot dead and her husband, the state governor, badly injured in Dallas, Texas, in 1963.

'Drill for oil? You mean drill into the ground to try and find oil? You're crazy' – Contractors that Edwin L. Drake tried to enlist for his project to drill for oil in 1859. On 27 August that year, Drake struck oil, the modern petroleum industry was founded and the world changed forever.

'Louis Pasteur's theory of germs is ridiculous fiction' – Pierre Pachet, professor of physiology at Toulouse, in 1872.

'Everything that can be invented has been invented' – Charles H. Duell, commissioner of the US Office of Patents, in 1899.

'It is not unlikely that Hitler will end his career as an old man in some Bavarian village who, in the beer garden in the evening, tells his intimates how he nearly overturned the German Reich. Strange battle cries will struggle to his lips and he will mention names that once trembled at his own name. But his neighbours will have heard this tale so often they will shrug their shoulders and bury their faces deeper into their mugs of Pilsner to hide their smiles. The old man, they will think, is entitled to his pipe dreams for it is comforting to live on the memory of an illusion' – Harold Laski writing in the *Daily Herald* in 1932, twelve weeks before Hitler overthrew the German Reich and became the chancellor of Germany.

'The modern house of the year 2000 will be waterproof both inside and out, so the lucky housewife can do all her cleaning with a hose' – *Popular Mechanics Magazine*, 1957.

'Houses will be able to fly by the year 2000. The time will come when whole communities may migrate south for the winter' – Arthur C. Clarke in 1967.

'We don't know yet' – The organizer of a convention of clairvoyants in Paris in 1978 replying to a question from a reporter about the following year's event.

'Damn it, Ma'am. I know your face but I cannot put a name to it' – Lord Portarlington on approaching Queen Victoria at a state reception.

'The United States has much to offer the Third World War' – Ronald Reagan addressing an international conference on issues concerning the Third World.

'Rail travel at high speed is not possible because passengers, unable to breathe, will die of asphyxia' – Dr Dionysius Lardner, professor of natural philosophy and astronomy at University College London, when plans were being drawn up for the great rail network in the early nineteenth century.

'The cinema is little more than a passing fad. What audiences really want to see is flesh and blood on the stage' – Charlie Chaplin.

'You had better learn how to type, or get married' – Blue Book Modelling Agency turning down Norma Jean Baker (Marilyn Monroe) in 1944.

THE BENEFITS OF HINDSIGHT: REMARKS MADE AND REGRETTED

INDEX OF STORY HEADINGS